New Zealand Wildlife

A VISITOR'S GUIDE

Julian Fitter

edition
I

www.bradtguides.com

Bradt Travel Guides Ltd, UK
The Globe Pequot Press Inc, USA

First published January 2009

Bradt Travel Guides Ltd
23 High Street, Chalfont St Peter, Bucks SL9 9QE, England
www.bradtguides.com
Published in the USA by The Globe Pequot Press Inc,
246 Goose Lane, PO Box 480, Guilford, Connecticut 06437-0480

British Library Cataloguing in Publication Data
A catalogue record for this book is available from the British Library

ISBN-13: 978 1 84162 272 9

Photographs
Heather Angel/Natural Visions (HA/NV), Arco Digital Images/Tips (AD/Tips),
Chromorange/Tips (C/Tips), Tui De Roy (TDR), J Kendrick/Department of Conservation,
New Zealand (JK/DOC), Tony Eldon (TE), Julian Fitter (JF), Neil Fitzgerald (NF),
Mark Jones (MJ), Angus McIntosh/Natural Sciences Image Library (AM/NSI),
Alexander Turnbull Library, Wellington, New Zealand (www.natlib.govt.nz/atl) (ATL),
Xcluder Pest Proof Fencing Company

Front cover Tui (TDR)
Back cover Tree weta (TDR)
Title page (from top to bottom)
Red-crowned parakeet (TDR); dusky dolphin (MJ); bulbinellas in spring (TDR)

Maps Malcolm Barnes

Designed and formatted by Pepenbury Ltd
Printed and bound in India at Nutech Photolithographers

DEDICATION For Jayne, who helped me explore and appreciate Aotearoa.

CONTENTS

ABOUT THE AUTHOR

Julian Fitter is a conservationist, naturalist and writer, with a special interest in island ecosystems and the battle to rid them of alien invaders. His first book, on Galapagos wildlife, was published in 2000, and is widely regarded as the best identification guide to the natural history of those islands.

In 1964 Julian sailed to the Galapagos Islands, where he founded the first yacht charter business. Then in 1977 he visited the Falkland Islands and became involved in developing tourism there. These experiences led to his work in conservation: in 1981 he was closely involved in establishing Falklands Conservation and served as its first secretary; in 1997 he also established the UK-based Galapagos Conservation Trust, where he was the first chairman and is now one of the ambassadors; and in 2006, with the help of local conservationists, he helped establish Friends of Galapagos New Zealand. He is also a vice president of Falklands Conservation.

Since 2005 Julian has been based in New Zealand, where he currently lives in the Bay of Plenty on North Island, writing books on natural history and helping the local conservation effort. He has visited several of the New Zealand sub-Antarctic islands, as well as Tristan da Cunha and Gough Island in the South Atlantic, and has become involved in their conservation through the Tristan Biodiversity Action Group.

ACKNOWLEDGEMENTS

My first thanks must be to Aotearoa – New Zealand – for being an amazing country with wonderful wildlife: such an easy place to write about. Thanks also to DOC (the Department of Conservation) and all their enthusiastic, energetic and dedicated staff. DOC manages over 30% of New Zealand and does a great job; without them there would be far less for the visitor to see. This book touches on a great variety of animals, plants, fungi and landforms, and consequently I needed help from many people, often on quite small matters. Among these were Jessica Beever, Trent Bell, Hugh Best, John Braggins, Thomas Buckley, Trish Fleming, Graeme Jane, Larry Jensen, Dave Kelly, Matthew Thorpe, Peter Newsome, Dave Row, Margaret Stanley, Rupert Sutherland, Maggie Wassilief, Janet Wilmshurst and Hugh Wilson. Apologies to anyone that I have missed. My thanks also to Tui De Roy, an old friend and neighbour from Galapagos, who provided most of the photographs and was responsible for me coming to New Zealand in the first place. I am grateful to Adrian Phillips and Mike Unwin at Bradt for putting up with my missed deadlines and very long text! Also to Mike Miles for his excellent design. My greatest thanks, however, must go to my partner, Jayne Ivimey, who put up with me hunched over my keyboard for endless hours, and provided continuous help, support, encouragement and solace.

INTRODUCTION

A UNIQUE WILDLIFE DESTINATION

New Zealand, or 'Aotearoa' to give it its Maori name, is a land of startling extremes and contrasts. Within just under 270,000km² the scenery shifts from snow-capped volcanoes, alpine peaks, glaciers and braided rivers to dense, luxuriant forests and wide, open tussock grasslands – in parts untouched by man, in others completely altered. All this is set in Mediterranean and subtropical latitudes, with over 15,000km of dramatic coastline surrounded by a cool ocean.

New Zealand broke away from the rest of Gondwana, the ancient supercontinent of the southern hemisphere, some 70–80 million years ago. As this occurred when mammal evolution was in its infancy, the only land mammals to make it to New Zealand were three species of bat. As a result, New Zealand became a land of birds, its wildlife quite unlike that of even its nearest neighbour Australia, a mere 2,300km to the west. New Zealand also enjoys a great diversity of plants – forest originally covered 80% of its surface. Thanks to its remote position it was the last major land mass (apart from Antarctica) to be colonised by man; the first Polynesian travellers did not arrive until about AD1250.

This guide deals mainly with the three main islands of the New Zealand archipelago – North Island, South Island and Stewart Island – as well as the inshore islands around their coasts. The more distant offshore islands, ranging from the subtropical Kermadecs in the north to the Chatham Islands to the east and the sub-Antarctic Auckland, Campbell and Antipodes groups 800km miles to the south, are hard to visit except on specialist cruises and so are not included other than in passing.

Inland New Zealand can be separated into three basic ecological areas: the coast and its associated wetlands, the forests from lowland to montane, and the high mountains with their bleak plateaux and snow-capped peaks. The coastline boasts miles and miles of sandy beaches, rugged rocky coasts and quiet tidal estuaries, with pristine forest or bush extending right down to the water's edge in many places.

Vegetable sheep and alpine daisies are among New Zealand's many unusual endemic alpine plants. TDR

At various points you can expect to see a number of marine mammals as well as a wide variety of sea, shore and wetland birds. If you venture offshore on a 'pelagic' wildlife-watching boat trip, you may encounter a variety of dolphins and whales, as well as many more seabirds.

In the forests, a dazzling variety of trees and plants makes for a wonderful canopy all year round. Here you could easily find two or three dozen different tree species in a hectare of woodland, compared with about half a dozen in a typical European or North American forest. Ferns grow in profusion, with more than 160 species, along with an array of mosses, liverworts and fungi. The forests are far from silent: there are places where you can still experience a dawn chorus of native New Zealand birds, holding forth with a truly wonderful variety of un-birdlike sounds that so impressed early visitors.

The tui is one of the most widespread of the native birds. MJ

Of the three main habitats, the alpine regions are probably the least affected by New Zealand's populations of non-native animals. There are over 600 species of alpine and sub-alpine plants, 93% of them found nowhere else in the world. You can enjoy a host of remarkable plants in the alpine areas, such as the bizarre woolly shrubs nicknamed 'vegetable sheep', which from a distance resemble a grazing flock of sheep. Birds are here too and so are the world's only known alpine lizards. And of course the scenery is to die for, be it massive glaciers, soaring peaks or dramatic symmetrical volcanic cones.

The actions of its human settlers have had a huge impact on the natural history of New Zealand, from the very first introduction of the Polynesian rat (kiore) some 750 years ago, through the havoc wreaked by the first Polynesian settlers to the giant, plant-eating moas and other flightless birds, to the zeal with which the European settlers of the 19th century hacked and burnt their way through the native forests. The Europeans compounded this damage by importing an amazing variety of animal species from their homelands and elsewhere, with devastating consequences for the native wildlife. This destruction has taken place in a relatively short space of time, but the tide has well and truly turned and New Zealand leads the world in its efforts to conserve what remains and reclaim what was lost, while large parts of the country remain a treasure-trove of natural beauty and fascinating diversity.

As this book is about New Zealand wildlife it will discuss introduced species only to emphasise the damage that they have done and are still doing to the native flora and fauna. Once you start to understand and appreciate the native species, you will see all the introduced trees, shrubs, grasses, herbaceous weeds, birds and mammals for what they are: alien invaders that simply do not belong.

So welcome to New Zealand, a country like no other in its wild beauty and unique flora and fauna. The natural biodiversity of Aotearoa is truly awe-inspiring. Enjoy it and appreciate it.

AOTEAROA – NEW ZEALAND

The Maori name for New Zealand, Aotearoa, means 'Land of the long white cloud', or 'long white day'. This is not how they referred to it before the arrival of the *pakeha* (the Maori term for the white Europeans). Maori did not see the New Zealand archipelago as a country, but as a number of islands. North Island was known to most of them as 'Te Ika a Maui' ('The Fish of Maui'). Some tribes called it 'Aoteo', though this was also the name of Great Barrier Island in the Hauraki Gulf, and the name Aotearoa was also sometimes used for just North Island. South Island was known as 'Te Waka-a-Aoraki' ('The Canoe of Aoraki') or 'Te Wahi Pounamou' ('The Place of Greenstone'), and Stewart Island was 'Rakiura' ('Glowing Skies').

The great spotted kiwi is the largest kiwi and occurs only on South Island. TDR

THE APPLIANCE OF SCIENCE

Scientists classify living things by a set of increasingly refined groupings, from the very general (eg: 'animal kingdom') down to each individual species and subspecies. Within the text of this book, we have included the scientific names of each plant and animal species or genus (plural genera), as well as English names. This avoids confusion, since you may find Maori names more widely used than English names, and the English names used in New Zealand for certain widespread species may be different from those the ones used in your part of world.

The scientific name of a species consists of a binomial (two-part) name, always in italic script, the first part indicating the genus, and the second part the species. These names are usually derived from Latin but also sometimes from ancient Greek or other languages. Sometimes a third name is added to make a trinomial name, and this indicates a subspecies of the species in question. Here are examples of the scientific classification down to species level for a bird and a plant:

The tuatara, a 'living fossil', can remain motionless for hours at a time. TDR

Australasian harrier

Kingdom	Animalia (animals)
Phylum	Chordata (vertebrates)
Class	Aves (birds)
Order	Falconiformes (birds of prey)
Family	Accipitridae (hawks and allies)
Genus	*Circus* (harriers)
Species	*Circus approximans* (Australasian harrier)

Kauri

Kingdom	Plantae (plants)
Division	Pinophyta (conifers, including extinct groups)
Class	Pinopsida (all living conifers)
Order	Pinales (pine trees)
Family	Araucariaceae
Genus	*Agathis* (kauris)
Species	*Agathis australis* (kauri)

WILDLIFE OVERVIEW

Every habitat in New Zealand has its own special wildlife. However, if you want to get acquainted with the native species quickly and easily, concentrate on the coast, the mountains or the bush, or combinations of these habitats. In the forests you will have tantalising glimpses of animals but perhaps not rewarding encounters, but in the mountains and around the coast the wildlife is rich, varied and much easier to see. If you are a birdwatcher on your first trip to New Zealand, then you should significantly add to your 'life list'. If you are a botanist, you will be in heaven. If you are neither, then you can simply enjoy the excitement of being in natural environments and among living creatures that are unlike anything you'll have experienced before.

In the absence of land mammals, birds evolved and diversified to occupy the traditional large-mammal roles of top predators and large plant-eaters; historically at least, birds held sway. Entomologists and lichen specialists might demur, however, as there are more than 6,000 species of beetle and 1,400 species of lichen compared with only around 250 original species of native bird.

THE COAST

The sea is fundamental to New Zealand life. There are 15,000km of coastline, which provides a vital habitat for the native wildlife – around 200 bird species, natives or regular visitors, depend on the shore or open sea. The southern fur seal and the New Zealand sea lion both breed on the coast and several other species of seal and sea lion occur from time to time. An impressive 38 species of whale and dolphin have been observed around the coast and there is a huge variety of other marine life: fish, rays, molluscs, seaweeds and corals abound in deep water, on rocks and in tidepools.

The northern royal albatross, which breeds near Dunedin, has the longest wingspan of any bird. TDR

The nature of the coast is very varied. There are remarkable 'pancake' layered rock formations at Punakaiki on the west coast of South Island, long sandy beaches with huge sand dunes as on 90 Mile Beach in Northland or Mason Bay on Stewart Island, teeming tidal pools around Wellington, ash and pumice cliffs in the Bay of Plenty and many quiet sheltered estuaries and harbours – nurseries for fish and havens for waders and other birds.

Hector's dolphin is found only in New Zealand. MJ

INSHORE AND OFFSHORE ISLANDS

While the New Zealand archipelago consists of three main islands, North, South and Stewart, together with over 100 smaller islands, there are a number of other offshore and inshore islands that are considered part of New Zealand. Most significant of the offshore islands are the Chatham Islands, some 800km east of Christchurch, which have a population of fewer than 1,000 people. The remaining offshore islands are the sub-tropical Kermadec Islands 1,000km to the northeast and the sub-Antarctic islands, Snares, Auckland, Campbell, Antipodes and Bounty islands to the south and southeast. All are uninhabited, and are important areas for seabirds, especially albatrosses and petrels. The sub-Antarctic islands form, collectively, a World Heritage Site, and all are difficult to visit except on special organised tours. It is relatively easy to fly to the Chathams, but getting to the seabird breeding areas is not possible without special permits.

The Pyramid in the Chatham Islands is the only place where Chatham albatrosses breed. TDR

The Kermadecs

The Kermadecs are an isolated group of volcanic islands, 1,000km north of New Zealand. They are the tips of submarine volcanoes and have never been linked to any other land mass. They have a sub-tropical climate, and thus a number of normally tropical birds such as noddies, boobies and tropicbirds breed there. Five of the 35 species of native bird are endemic, including the rare Kermadec petrel, as are 23 of the 113 native species and sub-species of plant. The islands are all nature reserves and all of the seas around them form the country's largest marine reserve, which covers the shallower water round the islands and the profound depths of the Kermadec Trench.

The yellow-eyed penguin is the largest native penguin. TDR

The inshore islands

New Zealand also has a large number of much closer inshore islands, especially to the east of North Island. Notable among these are the Three Kings, 50km to the northeast of Cape Reinga – well known for their wildlife and with a considerable degree of endemism. The Poor Knights off Northland, and Great and Little Barrier islands and Tiritiri Matangi in the Hauraki Gulf are also important wildlife areas. There are several islands in the Bay of Plenty: Mayor or Tuhua Island and Whale or Moutohora Island are both nature reserves and White Island off Whakatane is the most active volcano in New Zealand. Further south there are few significant islands, though Kapiti on the west coast north of Wellington is an important bird sanctuary.

THE FORESTS

There is still around 50,000km² of native bush or forest in New Zealand, making this by far the most important single natural habitat. It varies from lowland and coastal forest through montane and sub-alpine scrublands. These zones are not clearly defined because New Zealand is a mountainous country 1,000 miles long from north to south, so there are all manner of variations depending on latitude and altitude. There are also significant climate differences between the east and west coasts, the latter being much wetter and generally milder than the former.

Much of this native forest is in national parks or other protected areas, and such sites offer a real insight into the native biological diversity, with a single-day tramp (hike) enabling you to see many different vegetation zones. Pureora Mountain in the centre of North Island is a particularly good example of this.

You do not, however, have to go far to appreciate the amazing variety. In any area of forest you may notice special aspects of the New Zealand tree and shrub flora: trees with clear juvenile stages that wait as teenagers for years before being allowed to grow up; the extraordinary tangle of the supplejack vine; and shrubs that grow in on themselves creating an impenetrable matrix.

The crown fern is a common and distinctive fern in lowland forest. TDR

Ferns are a major feature of the bush, from the tall and majestic manuka tree fern which grows to a height of 12m or more, to the wonderful hen and chicken fern, which grows plantlets on its graceful fronds, and the delicate translucent 'filmy ferns' found on moist banks and streamsides. Here too you will find ancient conifers, podocarps including rimu and totara, and the amazing kauri, a member of the Araucariaceae family. This awesome tree, with its massive column-like trunk and crown of branches, is worth the trip to New Zealand alone.

THE MOUNTAINS

Both North and South islands are dominated by mountain chains, with extensive alpine areas on both islands, especially in the south. This has resulted in a very distinctive alpine and sub-alpine flora and fauna developing, with over 600 plant species as well as numerous unusual vertebrates and invertebrates. Fortunately most of the introduced alien species find life in the alpine zones too tough and so native species are still in the ascendancy here, though climate change is a threat.

Alpine plants include some groups you may know from your own gardens and others that will be quite new to you. There are hebes, some looking more like moss; tiny-leaved coprosmas, members of the coffee family; a remarkable variety of daisies and gentians; and an array of cushion plants including the woolly 'vegetable sheep'. All are well adapted to this harsh environment. On the animal front you have the inquisitive kea, the world's only alpine parrot, with its predilection for vandalising unattended human belongings. Here too is the diminutive rock wren, which spends its entire life above the tree line, as well as alpine grasshoppers, giant land snails, the wetas – unique and rather alarming-looking New Zealand insects which look like large ferocious grasshoppers – and, most surprising of all, a number of alpine skinks and geckos, the only truly alpine reptiles found anywhere.

Most of the native flora and much of the fauna is endemic – found nowhere else in the world – so on your first visit to New Zealand you can expect to encounter a huge range of creatures and plants you haven't seen before: from the iconic kiwi to the ancient tuatara lizard; from the nectar-eating, shiny-feathered tui to the elegant and lordly royal albatross; from whales and dolphins to parrots and fur seals. New Zealand is a new world, an ancient world, a different world.

New Zealand edelweiss is a member of the daisy family. TDR

WHERE TO GO – NORTH OR SOUTH?

While it may appear that South Island has more to offer in the way of natural history than North Island, this is not really true. There is certainly more untouched wilderness in the south, but the north has a lot to offer in the forests and forest parks, thermal areas and a more varied and accessible coastline. Also, with such accessible sanctuaries as Tiritiri Matangi, Kapiti and Somes islands, Maungatautari and Karori, it is easier to see many of the native birds in the north than in the south.

HUMAN HISTORY

We cannot be absolutely certain, but the earliest date of man's arrival in New Zealand appears to have been around 750 years ago. The first settlers were East Polynesians who arrived, according to oral tradition, in a fleet of 12 large canoes (*wakas*). They initially settled along the northeast coast of North Island, but soon spread to South and Stewart islands and to the Chathams.

Abel Tasman, a Dutchman who was searching for the great southern continent '*Terra australis ingognita*', was the first European to discover New Zealand. He landed in Golden Bay in the northwest of South Island on 13 December 1642, but had an unfortunate encounter with the local Maori and left having made little or no exploration of the country. No Europeans visited New Zealand for the next 127 years, until in 1769 James Cook on HMS *Endeavour* made landfall near Gisborne on the east coast of North Island. He too, having observed the Transit of Venus in Tahiti, was searching for the great southern continent.

While Tasman's discovery made little impact, Cook's visit, the first of three, was significant. He circumnavigated the country and made remarkably accurate charts of virtually the whole coastline. His account of the voyage, together with specimens (and detailed descriptions) of the flora and fauna made by Joseph Banks, a future president of the Royal Society, and Daniel Solander, a pupil of Carl Linnaeus, put New Zealand and its natural history on the map both literally and figuratively. Sydney Parkinson's detailed sketches, drawings and paintings from the trip are much admired to this day.

CAPTAIN COOK.

Captain James Cook was the first European to explore and chart New Zealand. ATL

10

CAPTAIN JAMES COOK

Cook was a remarkable and able seaman and navigator, and he was also concerned about developing good relations with indigenous peoples. He made three voyages to New Zealand; the first, in 1869, had taken him initially to Tahiti to observe the Transit of Venus. When he left there in search of '*Terra australis incognita*', he brought with him Tupaea, a Tahitian chief, as an interpreter to help deal with any indigenous people that he might encounter. Even so his first encounters with Maori were not successful, but on this first visit he circumnavigated the islands and produced a set of remarkably accurate charts. He made two further voyages, visiting New Zealand in 1773 and 1777. It was his favourable reports that attracted first sealers and whalers and later settlers to New Zealand. Joseph Banks and Daniel Solander accompanied Cook on his first trip, and were the first to describe the native fauna and flora.

It was not long before commerce arrived. Cook's voyages had revealed the wealth of natural resources. The first arrivals were whalers and sealers, followed by loggers attracted by the apparently limitless supply of tall, straight trees, in particular the kauri, which were much in demand for ships' spars. The Maori also traded flax, providing them with the means to obtain European goods such as knives and muskets. This period, from about 1790 through to 1840, was marked by generally good and cordial relations between the pakeha, the Maori term for Europeans, and the Maori. There was considerable commercial involvement, few if any conflicts and quite a lot of intermarriage.

Britain was initially unwilling to take on responsibility for New Zealand, but eventually agreed to, and the Treaty of Waitangi was signed on 6 February 1840, initially by some 45 Maori chiefs, and subsequently by more than 500 throughout the country. This marked the start of a new era but also started a debate about the precise interpretation of the treaty that continues to this day.

In 1840 there were only some 2,000 *pakeha* living in New Zealand; by 1881, there were 500,000, a remarkable migration especially given the distances and hardships

involved. Most of these settlers were coming to find a new life, and they needed land, most of which was in the hands of the Maori. This, unsurprisingly, led to a fair amount of friction and eventually armed skirmishes and war. The conflicts went on until 1881; during this period the Maori lost much land and developed a long-standing distrust for the government.

During this period, the economy grew and developed. It was originally based on coal, timber and gold, but

Cook's ship on his first voyage to New Zealand was HMS *Endeavour*, a converted coal-carrier. ATL

11

PAKEHA AND MAORI

The original settlers of New Zealand did not have a word to refer to themselves as a distinct people. Their social structure was divided into *iwi* or tribes, *hapu* or sub-tribes and *whanau* or family. The term Maori translates as 'people' and the Treaty of Waitangi in 1840 refers to the original inhabitants as *tangata maori* or 'ordinary people'.

The term 'pakeha' was used by the Maori to refer to the Europeans and was not in any sense disrespectful. It was used in 1840 in the Treaty of Waitangi to refer to Queen Victoria's non-Maori subjects. It may stem from the term *pakepakeha*, denoting mythical white-skinned beings.

The Treaty of Waitangi between the Maori and the British was signed in 1840 and is still in force, used to resolve outstanding land ownership disputes. ATL

developed into an agricultural one supplemented by the older industries. The discovery of gold had brought yet more settlers, including people from China and other Asian countries. Sheep farming developed as a major industry – the first shipment of frozen mutton was sent to Britain in 1877, reducing the country's previous reliance on exporting only the non-perishable wool, the price of which was very variable.

Parliamentary government started in 1853, and the country ceased to be a colony and became a self-governing dominion within the British Empire in 1907.

Full independence was granted in 1947. The Liberal government of 1890 introduced many social reforms; large land holdings were broken up and communities began to build libraries and schools. In 1893 New Zealand became the first country in the world to give women the vote. The following year saw the introduction of the world's first compulsory arbitration system for industrial disputes, setting the tone for the country as being at the forefront of social thinking and development that has influenced its governance ever since.

New Zealanders were much involved with both world wars, leaving their mark and their blood at Gallipoli, the Somme and Passchendaele in the first, and Egypt and Monte Casino among others in the second. Since then the country has continued to develop a strong economy based on industrial agriculture, with all its problems, and extractive industries, especially forestry and coal, supplemented more recently by technology and tourism. While strong links remain with Britain, the focus of the country has been increasingly towards its Pacific neighbours, especially Australia, China and Japan.

Today the population is mixed and cosmopolitan. Just over four million people live in New Zealand, with over 30% living in the Auckland area and only a million in the whole of South Island. While the bulk of the population is still of European descent, an increasing number of immigrants are from Asia. Precisely what this will mean for the future is unclear, but for the moment New Zealand is free from some of the problems of many developed countries where ethnic and religious tensions are high and society is under serious strain.

MAORI CULTURE AND LAND

When Captain Cook first encountered the Maori, they had what was essentially a stone-age culture, with no metal implements or vessels. They had, however, developed an advanced social culture. Central to every Maori's cultural identity is *whakapapa* or genealogy: knowing who your *atua* (ancestors) were is necessary to know who you are. The concept of *taonga* is key to understanding this. Taonga can either be a physical object, such as a cloak or a greenstone weapon, or can be intangible, such as the knowledge of how to carve or to sing a lament. As taonga is passed through the generations it becomes more valuable. Also important in Maori culture is *mana*, which translates as prestige, dignity, power or influence, and denotes the spiritual force in the person, which is inherited at birth from the *atua*.

While early European settlers fitted in with Maori culture, later settlers – right through until the late 20th century – did much to suppress and discourage it, including banning the use of Maori language in schools. Maori culture is now experiencing a resurgence, which bodes well for the conservation of New Zealand's cultural as well as its ecological heritage.

Maori is not the easiest of languages to get your tongue around. It uses a small alphabet with a lot of repeated syllables, and virtually all words end in a vowel. Vowels are pronounced as in Spanish: *ah, eh, ee, oh, oow*; and there is no emphasis on any syllable – or if at all on the first. The letters *wh* are pronounced more as a soft *f*. (See page 181.)

CONSERVATION

The New Zealand ecosystem evolved in isolation and, before the arrival of man, was unlike any other. The forested, mountainous islands are set in a warm-temperate to Mediterranean climate zone, but are somewhat protected from temperature extremes by their oceanic location. As already mentioned, the absence of land mammals led to the evolution of a unique and unusual birdlife.

The impact that man has had on this unique fauna has been dramatic and rapid. The first Polynesian settlers exterminated the moas and other flightless birds, bringing rats and dogs and using fire to clear the forests. The European settlers were much more efficiently destructive: they used machinery to level the forests and drain the wetlands, and brought a new generation of non-native animals with them. Since the arrival of man, New Zealand has lost some 41 species of bird, including more than a third of its land birds.

Right up until just 40 years ago, the prevailing mindset was to get the most, in financial terms, out of the land, and that effectively meant destroying the forests or draining the wetlands for what they could provide. Settlers brought in alien animal species by accident but also deliberately for financial gain – to provide food, skins and hunting, and even to try and control previously introduced species that had become a problem. More than 30 species of alien land mammal have been introduced to New Zealand, probably the most destructive being the brush-tailed possum from Tasmania, followed closely by the stoat, ferret, domestic goat and various rats.

Information boards are widely used in DOC and other conservation areas. TDR

14

Fortunately the prevailing mood shifted in the 1970s and, while there is still some resistance, most New Zealanders are supportive of efforts to get rid of alien species and restore native forests – although the farming, hunting and fishing lobbies are powerful and broad-based, so compromises are needed.

The big step forward came in 1987 when the Department of Conservation (DOC) was established, bringing together skills from several other government agencies to provide a single agency. DOC's role was to protect natural and historic heritage, and to provide recreational opportunities on land entrusted to its care. Nature was to be protected for its own sake and for future generations to enjoy.

Over the past 20 years, DOC and other government agencies and NGOs such as the Royal Forest & Bird Protection Society, the Ornithological Society of New Zealand and smaller local groups have managed to turn things around. Today, these agencies have made New Zealand the world leader in the eradication of alien pest species. They have established a number of predator-free islands, and by developing sophisticated pest-eradication techniques have helped create predator-free sanctuaries on the main islands. By developing and maintaining a network of campsites, trails and overnight huts, they have also enabled millions of people to experience the New Zealand wilderness in a safe and environmentally friendly way.

More good news comes in the form of forest and wetland restoration schemes, often with assistance from DOC, such as those on Titritiri Matangi and Kapiti islands, and at the private Hinewai Reserve on the Banks Peninsula and at Raketu Wetlands in Southland. Possibly the most ambitious is the Maungatautari Ecological Island near Cambridge, where a 47km predator-proof fence has been constructed. These projects and others like them are making a significant contribution to the re-establishment of New Zealand's biological diversity.

While things have improved, conservationists can never relax. They must develop ever-newer techniques and technologies to remove and control invasive species. However, the basic argument has been won and, while extinct species will never return and some alien pests may never be removed, there is a likelihood that in 20 years' time it will be easier to see and hear New Zealand's native species than it is now.

FENCED OUT

New Zealand has many nasty alien species that it has no chance of getting rid of completely. Conservationists have come up with two exclusion strategies designed to help preserve its native wildlife. The first is the establishment of alien-free island sanctuaries, such as those on Tiritiri Matangi and Kapiti. The second is the creation of so-called 'inland islands', such as Karori and Maungatautari. To create these reserves, a fencing system is used to keep out ground-dwelling alien predator species. Not only does the mesh have to be very fine and durable, but it has to be set a metre into the ground and to have a skirt extending out from the fence for another metre to deter burrowing animals. The top overhangs outwards and has a smooth curved edge, rather like upside-down guttering, to stop climbers getting in.

New Zealand has pioneered the use of pest-proof fencing to protect endangered native species.

NATIONAL PARKS AND OTHER PROTECTED AREAS

New Zealand has a large and, at first sight, complex system of national parks and protected areas. The total land conservation area totals nearly eight million hectares, with a further 1.1 million hectares of marine protected areas. Much of this is managed by the Department of Conservation (DOC), which is responsible for the management of some 30% of the country.

The system for categorising natural protected areas is bewildering. Seventeen different land categories exist, covered by four separate acts of parliament. A further four marine categories are covered by another four parliamentary acts. **Nature reserve** is the highest category of protected area – in most cases ordinary visitors are not allowed to visit such sites at all and if visits are allowed they are strictly controlled. **National parks** are fully protected but access is generally good and visitors are encouraged, while **forest parks** are somewhat lower down the priority list and some additional commercial and recreational activities are allowed in them. At the other end of the scale are local **recreational** and **scenic reserves**, which are often quite small. All of these designations offer a degree of protection and access, and even quite small areas of native bush and wetland are often well worth a visit. There are also a number of private reserves outside the government system: Karori Sanctuary in Wellington, Hinewai on the Banks Peninsula, Tawharanui near Warkworth, Raketu Wetlands in Southland and Maungatautari Ecological Island in the Waikato are good examples.

Tongariro in central North Island, with its trio of volcanos, was the first national park, established in 1887 when Te Heuheu Tukino IV (Horonuku), the paramount chief of Ngati Tuwharetoa, gifted the sacred peaks to the nation. There are now 13 national parks, mostly on South Island, but there are 20 forest parks, with more in the north than the south.

National parks and other protected areas are generally administered and managed by DOC. They maintain a network of high-quality tramping or hiking tracks, as well as many excellent back-country and mountain huts. While booking these is not essential, it is wise to do so on popular tramps and at busy times of the year, especially from Christmas through to the end of January. For some routes, such as the Milford Track in Fiordland, numbers are restricted and you have to book well in advance.

NATIONAL PARKS
North Island
Te Urewera, Tongariro, Whanganui, Egmont
South Island
Abel Tasman, Kahurangi, Paparoa, Nelson Lakes, Arthur's Pass, Westland, Mount Cook, Mount Aspiring, Fiordland
Stewart Island
Rakiura

WORLD HERITAGE SITES
New Zealand has three World Heritage sites. This designation does not add anything to the protected status of the areas concerned, but raises their profile in conservation terms.

- **Tongariro National Park** comprises the three active volcanoes Ruapehu, Ngauruhoe and Tongariro in North Island. This is a dual WHS due to its cultural significance to Maori.
- **Te Wāhipounamu – South West New Zealand World Heritage Area** comprises the Fiordland, Mount Aspiring, Westland and Aoraki Mount Cook National Parks, representing some 10% of New Zealand's land area.
- **The sub-Antarctic islands of New Zealand** comprises several island groups to the south and east of New Zealand: The Snares, Bounty, Antipodes, Auckland and Campbell islands.

Visiting the first two is straightforward, but the third is only possible as part of an organised tour and even then there is no access to some islands and limited access on others.

Two more natural areas have been proposed for World Heritage status: the Kermadec Islands and Marine Reserve to the north of New Zealand; and Kahurangi National Park and Farewell Spit at the northwest tip of South Island.

ALIEN INVASION

Oceanic islands, because of their isolation, almost always accommodate a restricted but very interesting community of plants and animals. Depending on how the island came into being, most of the animals that become established there will have arrived under their own steam, and so the ecosystem develops in a very individual way. The Galapagos Islands, Hawaii and Madagascar provide good examples of distinctive island fauna. Such ecosystems are extremely vulnerable to the introduction of new species that are accustomed to making their livings in much more diverse and competitive environments.

New Zealand had a pristine natural environment until about 750 years ago. All the living things on the islands had reached them by their own efforts or through natural forces, mainly wind and ocean currents. The first humans to arrive were Polynesians who brought with them man's two eternal companions, the Polynesian rat or kiore, and the dog.

Life in New Zealand has not been the same since the rats came. The native New Zealand animals had no way to defend themselves against the sudden mass arrival of these tough, adaptable predators, and their arrival was the start of a steady and, in some cases, terminal decline of many of New Zealand's invertebrates, reptiles and land birds. In the case of birds, a third were either flightless or had limited powers of flight, making them particularly vulnerable.

The humans, whom we now know as Maori, stayed and further modified the ecosystem through land clearance and hunting the flightless birds – especially the moas. The arrival of the Europeans in the late 18th century accelerated this process. These new arrivals brought advanced technologies and large numbers of invasive species, especially mammals, including rats, pigs, cats, stoats, goats and rabbits.

While modest efforts were made from the late 19th century onwards to protect some native species, the technology did not exist to eradicate the predators and so little progress was made until the 1960s and 1970s. Public opinion became overwhelmingly concerned with the native versus alien animals issue, and at the same time technology was developed, in the forms of effective poisons, helicopters and all-terrain vehicles, to really make an impact.

Some alien species have had little adverse impact, but have thrived because the environment has been changed. Most native land birds lived in the forest. As the trees disappeared, the birds lost their habitat and food sources and became restricted to the reduced areas of forest that remained. Meanwhile, introduced starlings, blackbirds and chaffinches, veterans of the European agricultural countryside and urban areas, prospered in the new landscapes of New Zealand. Other aliens proved extremely destructive, particularly stoats and ferrets. These predators were themselves imported in the hope that they would control other non-native animals – the rabbit and the brush-tailed possum. However, no-one explained to the stoats and ferrets that they should concentrate their efforts on eating their fellow aliens, and New Zealand's native wildlife took another battering.

Nor did the settlers bring just mammals and birds. New Zealand also harbours more than 22,000 species of non-native plants, and countless invertebrates.

It would appear that the European settlers were hell-bent on removing all traces of the native flora and fauna and replacing them with more familiar plants and animals. As late as the 1970s there were societies dedicated to the introduction of new species, and many gardeners and horticulturalists still appear to be blind to the dangers.

left The brush-tailed possum from Tasmania is one of the most numerous and destructive pest species in New Zealand. TDR

below Possum research in action. TDR

Gorse is an invasive and problematic alien species, but is now often used as a nursery plant for native bush regeneration projects. JF

DOC spends millions of dollars annually controlling over 300 weed species that threaten the integrity of over 600,000ha of protected areas, quite apart from its battle against introduced mammals. Farmers and foresters spend more millions attacking weeds and pests – water weeds are a serious problem in hydro-generating plants and a severe threat to freshwater fisheries.

As a result of this battle against alien invaders, New Zealand has developed an impressive ability and an array of technology to deal with unwanted new arrivals. Both its experts and expertise are in demand worldwide to help in eradication and control programmes. Its bio-security system is second to none.

BIO-SECURITY

Bio-security is a serious issue in New Zealand. You are not allowed to import ANY plant or animal material into New Zealand without a permit, apart from obviously risk-free items such as woollen or leather clothing and equipment. Even a can of cooked fruit or a candy bar can earn you an on-the-spot-fine on arrival if it is not declared. Any natural item sent by post may be opened and destroyed. I was once sent a card containing a single leaf – this was detected, opened and destroyed. (We could have paid a large fee to have it treated.) On another occasion I was fined NZ$200 for bringing in two kiwi fruit that I had forgotten about! Given the problems caused here by alien species, these precautions are entirely reasonable and understandable.

THE LAND

Mount Cook and the rapidly retreating Tasman Glacier.

The dramatic and varied landscape of New Zealand is one of its biggest draws as a tourist destination. It is popular with film directors looking for a magnificent natural canvas against which to set their stories – the *Lord of the Rings* trilogy directed by Peter Jackson (himself a New Zealander) is a well-known recent example. So much scenery is packed into the relatively small land area of the islands that the massive popularity of walking (tramping) and outdoor sports is hardly surprising.

GEOGRAPHY AND GEOLOGY

The most obvious features of the physical geography of New Zealand are its mountains. There are the impressive Southern Alps, the spine of South Island, and the eastern ranges and spectacular volcanoes of North Island. New Zealand is also a country replete with lakes and rivers, flat coastal plains and a varied and at times spectacular coastline. It has three main islands: North, South and Stewart. These, along with some 700 inshore and offshore islands, are the tips of a huge submarine plateau, the New Zealand continent or Zealandia, which gives the country a very extensive economic zone out of all proportion to the land area of the archipelago.

THE ROCKS

Most of the rocks that form South Island are of non-volcanic origin, with just three small areas of volcanic (igneous) rocks, namely Banks Peninsula near Christchurch, Dunedin and west Otago. In the north there are some particularly good examples of weathered or karst limestone at Takaka Hill in Nelson. North Island is also composed largely of non-volcanic rocks, including some immensely thick mudstone deposits. The noted glow-worm caves at Waitomo are in limestone. On top of these are often thick deposits of ash and pumice from the very active volcanic area, which

Fox Glacier on the west coast of South Island flows to within 20km of the sea. JF

Ruapehu, at 2,797m, is the highest peak on North Island and has regular eruptions. This one was in 1996. TDR

stretches from the Central Plateau through Taupo and Rotorua to the Bay of Plenty and Coromandel. Taranaki in the west is a snow-capped volcano and Auckland is built around nine volcanoes.

THE TOPOGRAPHY

The towering Southern Alps dominate South Island. These, together with the Spencer and Richmond ranges in Nelson and Marlborough, run its entire length. To the west is a very narrow coastal strip and to the east lies an upland plateau and a broad, flat, coastal plain. The beautiful and complex braided rivers, a mile or more wide, are characteristic of the east, as are the deep glacial lakes. Another feature of South Island's landscape is the amount of glaciation – there are notable glaciers around Mount Cook, and the Fox and Franz Joseph glaciers on the west coast flow to within 10km of the sea. A flight over the region provides not only breathtakingly beautiful views but a wonderful lesson in glaciology.

The North Island has a more varied geography, with a complex series of geological fault-lines running up from Wellington to the Bay of Plenty. To the east there is a coastal plain, though not as flat as its equivalent in South Island. The Tararua, Ruahine, Kaweka, Huiarau, Kahikatea and Raukama ranges form a near-continuous spine running from Wellington to East Cape, with only five routes across its 550km length. To the west of this ridge is the largest area of volcanics in New Zealand. The Central Plateau and its magnificent active volcanoes of Ruapehu, Ngauruhoe and Tongariro, are further enhanced by the lakes of Taupo, Rotorua, Tarawera, Rotoiti and Rotoma. The whole region around Rotorua is full of amazing thermal attractions: geysers, hot springs, hot baths, mud baths, boiling mud and nine geothermal power stations. On the west coast is the beautiful, symmetrical volcanic cone of Mount Taranaki. In the north, Auckland is built on a volcanic area featuring at least nine (hopefully extinct) volcanoes.

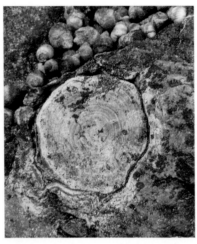

Tree growth rings in the fossil forest at Curio Bay. JF

THE COAST

New Zealand is a seaside-lover's dream, with miles of sandy beaches alternating with rugged bush-clad rocky coasts. Among the special features are 90 Mile Beach in Northland; the shallow tidal flats in the Firth of Thames, featuring one of the few Chenier beaches (made up of millions of mollusc shells from the mudflats of the Firth of Thames) in the southern hemisphere at Miranda; and the rugged coasts of Coromandel and the East Cape. In South Island there are the Moeraki Boulders, giant spherical boulders revealed by the erosion of the mudstone cliffs; the amazing fossilised forest at Curio Bay on the Catlins coast; the dramatically beautiful Milford Sound in Fiordland; and the strange stacked limestone formations known as 'pancake' rocks at Punakaiki on the west coast.

The Moeraki Boulders are large spherical boulders that have eroded out of the soft mudstone cliffs. JF

Milford Sound, in the heart of Fiordland, is one of New Zealand's greatest scenic attractions. TDR

SETTLEMENT

This very varied geography has resulted in a distinct divide, with inland areas being either farmland or wilderness and the human population concentrated around the coast. Five of the six largest cities – Auckland, Wellington, Tauraunga, Christchurch and Dunedin – are on the coast, with Hamilton, south of Auckland, the only major inland urban area. Of the total population of 4.2 million, over 65% live in the four coastal cities and their regions, and less than 25% of the population lives on South Island, even though it is significantly larger at 150,000km^2 than North Island at 114,000km^2. This equates to a density of under seven people per square kilometre on South Island, and more than 27 on North Island. Another interesting statistic is that 84% of New Zealanders live in urban areas, one of the highest levels in the world.

THE HISTORY OF THE LAND

The land that we now know as New Zealand has had a very varied history and has only quite recently taken its present form. After New Zealand separated from Gondwana between 70 and 80 million years ago, the next 35 million years brought a combination of erosion and rising sea levels, especially a period known as the 'Oligocene Drowning' some 25 million years ago. This left the country as a series of small, scattered islands. Since then sea levels have fallen, and at the height of the last ice age some 20,000 years ago, New Zealand was one large island. The impact of the glaciers during that ice age, along with tectonic plate movements and volcanic eruptions, have all helped to form the country that we see today.

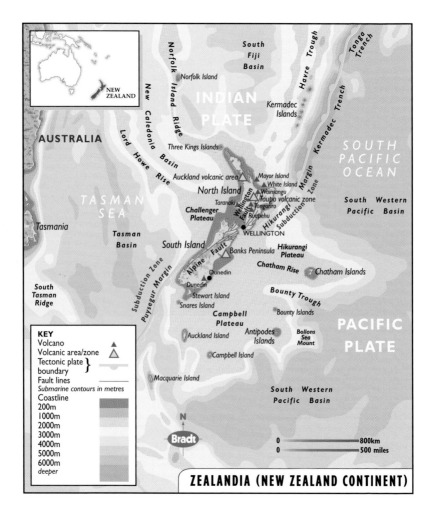

ZEALANDIA (NEW ZEALAND CONTINENT)

FROZEN IN TIME

The last ice age was at its height some 20,000 years ago and is reckoned to have ended about 14,000 years ago. At its height an ice sheet covered the whole of the Southern Alps, with relatively modest ice fields on Taranaki and the central volcanoes on North Island. The alpine zone was also much more extensive at this time, especially in Otago. It reached almost to the present-day coast near Dunedin, and on North Island included most of the east coast ranges. Along with the growth of the ice caps, the sea level fell some 120m below its present level so that all three islands were united. The Waikato River, which now meets the sea on the west coast south of Auckland, exited on the east coast north of Auckland. Forests were confined largely to the northwest of North Island and a small part of what is now northwest South Island. The current vegetation system has developed since then.

THE FAULTS

New Zealand is a very young country and is geologically very active, with tectonic faults, volcanoes, glaciers and rivers all building and eroding the land at the same time.

The country sits astride the meeting place of the Pacific and Australian tectonic plates, and this tumultuous location has played a major part in the formation of the islands. The junction of the plates, which is known as the Alpine Fault, runs from Fiordland in the southwest of South Island right through to the Bay of Plenty in North Island. For most of South Island it is a clearly visible single fault but north of Christchurch it splits and a number of smaller faults run up through Wellington and eastern North Island, and then offshore along the Kermadec Trench. This fault has over the past 25 million years pushed up the Southern Alps an amazing 20,000m – only erosion has kept the peaks below 4,000m. The Alpine Fault is moving at some 30mm per year; rocks just south of Nelson used to be 460km further south in Westland. To the north the Pacific plate is pushed under the Indo-Australian plate, and this is partly responsible for the very active volcanic area around Taupo and Rotorua.

These faults result in many earthquakes, some 10,000–15,000 a year. Only 10% of the tremors are noticeable, but each year also brings several magnitude 6 quakes, the level at which significant damage may be caused. A major quake of magnitude 8 or more has occurred four times in the last 900 years, the last one in 1717 – geologists expect another within the next 40 years or so. The faults are responsible for the Napier earthquake of 1931 that destroyed the town, and for the 1855 Wairapa quake that uplifted the Wellington cricket ground, the Basin Reserve – which had previously been earmarked as a shipping basin – and the shelf on which both the railway and main road north out of Wellington now run.

THE VOLCANOES

Not only is New Zealand earthquake country, it is also volcano country, with four large active volcanoes. White Island in the Bay of Plenty is the most active volcano but is significantly smaller. The most recent major eruptions have been on Mount Ruapehu, with a sizeable one in 1996 and smaller ones in 2006 and 2007. Mount Taranaki in the east is due a major eruption, but the biggie, when it comes, is likely to be at

Taupo. This has a history of massive eruptions, primarily of ash and pumice, thanks in part to the presence of Lake Taupo, as the combination of water and super-hot magma makes for a very explosive eruption producing ash and pumice rather than lava. The last big eruption occurred 1,800 years ago and devastated 20,000km^2 of North island, but the real blowout was 26,500 years ago, an eruption that produced 800km^3 of material, covering the whole of New Zealand with a thick layer of volcanic material. You can see these stratified layers of ash and pumice in road cuttings throughout the central North Island as well as in the coastal cliffs on the eastern Bay of Plenty.

THE THERMAL REGION

The thermal region around Rotorua is one of the big attractions in New Zealand, though the smell can be a little off-putting; when the wind is in the south you can smell the sulphur on the coast 50km away. At Waimangu you can walk down a valley with hot lakes, mud pools, silica terraces and vegetation that have developed from nothing over the last 150 years. This valley was formed overnight on 10 June 1886 when Mount Tarawera blew up, covering much of North Island in mud and ash, destroying a village and devastating the area around the volcano. Other sites in the area offer geysers, hot pools, coloured pools, hot mud baths and, above all, the ever-present smell.

The water level of Inferno Crater at Waimangu near Rotorua changes constantly on a regular but varied cycle. JF

PALAEONTOLOGY

New Zealand has a rich collection of fossil and sub-fossil remains, which is not surprising given that much of the country is made up of slowly formed, sedimentary rocks. Finding fossils is not difficult. You will frequently travel on roads cut into mudstone or other soft sedimentary material and in the banks you should easily find fossils, although they have an annoying tendency to fall to pieces as they dry. These are most likely of marine life, particularly fairly recent (geologically speaking) fossils of shells, and perhaps also the occasional leaf. In the Bay of Plenty you can find burnt wood and charcoal embedded in the cliffs, souvenirs of the many cataclysmic eruptions experienced over the millennia.

The fossil record has been an important indicator of the gradual development of New Zealand, from a slice of Gondwana to its present isolated circumstances. Future discoveries will no doubt reveal more of the history of the country.

Impressive cloud formations at Golden Bay on South Island. TDR

CLIMATE AND WEATHER

Perfect blue skies, startlingly clear visibility, inspirational sunrises, rapturous sunsets, torrential downpours, hurricane-force winds...these are some of the meteorological experiences on offer in New Zealand, resulting from an unusual climate, best described as 'Oceanic Mediterranean'. The country's range and variety of climates and microclimates are remarkable, influenced very considerably by its mountainous geography and oceanic location. The country extends from the subtropical climate at latitude 36°S in the north, to 47°S where the climate is distinctly temperate. Altitude, the proximity of mountains and the ocean create moderating influences that produce a wide range of microclimates. The major weather systems affecting the country are a series of large low-pressure systems coming from the west, and in the late summer and autumn tropical cyclones, which come from the east, and which generally but not invariably pass to the north of the country.

In very general terms the further north you go the warmer the weather, and the further west the wetter. However, while the mountains attract rainfall they have

Aoraki Mount Cook, 3,754m, is New Zealand's highest mountain and is being constantly uplifted and eroded. MJ

rain-shadows (dry regions) on the sides facing away from the prevailing wind. Rainfall varies from over 12m per year in mountainous areas along the west coast of South Island, to under 400mm in central and eastern South Island. North Island has rather more homogenous rainfall patterns, in line with its generally less dramatic topography, with the highest rainfalls being around 3m on the higher ground, especially in the west, and lows of around 800–1,000mm mainly in southern and eastern areas. The hottest, coldest, wettest and driest records are all held by South Island.

New Zealand's wide range of climates, from subtropical in the far north to oceanic temperate in the south – with its myriad microclimates in between – has had a huge impact on shaping its wildlife communties. There are technically 17 different climate zones, all of which will result in a different ecosystem, and each has given rise to distinct species of animals and plants. In climate terms, New Zealand is not just three islands, since each of the three is divided into many, much smaller, climatic and ecological 'islands'.

WHEN TO VISIT

As with many places, winter (June to August) is not the best time to visit, especially North Island, where it is the wettest period almost everywhere. South Island is generally wetter in the spring (September to November) though the far south is wettest in autumn (March to May). The alpine areas are really only accessible in late spring through early autumn. As befits an oceanic climate, the weather is very changeable with severe weather closing in very quickly at times and being difficult to forecast, so apply the precautionary principle if you are venturing into the wilderness; in particular make sure that someone knows your plans and take a mobile phone.

Habitats

Beech Forest, Haast JF

Farewell Spit on South Island is a wildlife sanctuary. TDR

New Zealand's habitats can be broken down into five main categories: coast (and associated wetlands); forest; lakes and rivers; alpine and sub-alpine; and agricultural and urban environments. There is considerable variation within these categories depending on altitude, latitude and rainfall.

THE COAST

New Zealand has a wide variety of coastal habitats but, apart from Fiordland in the southwest, there are surprisingly few sections of coast with really sizeable rocky cliffs. However, there are many sections of rocky coast and numerous rocky headlands and promontories. Over a third of the coastline is made up of either sand or shingle beaches. Also common are low cliffs composed of mudstone or other soft sedimentary material, which is often eroding rapidly. A good example of this is at Moeraki on the east coast of South Island where the large spherical Moeraki Boulders are emerging one by one from the mudstone cliffs.

SANDY BEACHES

In general large sand beaches are not especially good for wildlife, but you will find a variety of waders and gulls scattered along them, in particular the variable and pied oystercatchers (*Haematopus unicolor* and *H. longirostris*) and red-billed and southern black-backed gulls (*Larus scopulinus* and *L. dominicanus*). Less visible are several species of edible shellfish, including surf clams such as the large toheroa (*Paphies ventricosa*) and two species of tuatua (*P. donacina* and *P. subtriangulata*), which favour open exposed beaches regularly pounded by heavy waves. Adult toheroas live just below the high-tide level, buried in the sand at depths of 20–30cm. Tuatuas prefer deeper water, living 5–10cm deep in the sand near the low-tide level. Closer to the surface, and betrayed by the small sand mounds they produce, are mantis shrimps (*Squilla armata*) and ghost shrimps (*Callianassa filholia*). You will find multitudes of sand-hoppers (*Talorchestia quoyana*) sheltering under dead seaweed. Keep an eye open also for pieces of pumice stone: this ultra-light volcanic rock is common on North Island, but on South Island may have come from an eruption a long way away.

SAND DUNES

Behind many of the sand beaches are extensive dune systems, especially on 90 Mile Beach in Northland, Mason Bay on Stewart Island, and the impressive 130km dune system in the South Taranaki Bight to the north of Wellington. New Zealand has around 1,100km of coastal sand dunes altogether, originally stretching as far as 19km inland and rising to a height of more than 150m. Dunelands now cover some 390km², only 30% of their original extent. The northernmost part of New Zealand, the Aupouri Peninsula, is a large area of dune lands.

Sand dunes comprise a very specialised ecosystem. The first plant colonisers here are two native creeping grasses, pingao (*Desmoschoenus spiralis*) and spinifex (*Spinifex sericeus*), both of which help to anchor the sand and provide an open habitat for other native species. The recently introduced marram grass (*Ammophila arenaria*) has become dominant in many areas and this grows much more densely, excluding other species of plant and invertebrates and changing the nature of the dunes. Other introduced and invasive plants that damage the dune ecosystem are the tree lupin (*Lupinus arboreus*) and Monterey pine (*Pinus radiata*). Birds that you may find here include the endangered New Zealand dotterel (*Chadrius obscurus*), the New Zealand pipit (*Anthus novaeseelandiae*) and the white-fronted tern (*Sterna striata*).

Where the native grasses survive, watch out for two endemic and mildly poisonous spiders: the katipo (*Latrodectus katipo*) has an orange-red stripe on its upper body and the black katipo (*L. atritus*) is all-black. Both species are endangered, due to habitat loss. Here too you may find the endemic sand scarab beetle (*Pericoptus truncatus*), which is black and shiny and up to 4cm long. Watch out also for middens, ancient Maori rubbish dumps, which can contain a wide variety of shells and bones.

Sand dunes are fragile and important environments, and important parts of the coastal defences, so please be careful and respect them, do not drive on them and where possible stay on existing trails.

There are long stretches of sand dunes all around the coasts. JF

ROCKY COASTS

On the rocky shorelines there is a rich variety of wildlife. At or above the high-tide mark you will find the banded periwinkle (*Austrolittorina antipodium*), with its small conical blue-and-white shell. Further down are the filter feeders: three species of mussels including the diminutive blue-black mussel (*Xenostrobus pulex*) and two common species of barnacle, the small column barnacle (*Chamaesipho columna*) and the much larger ridged barnacle (*Eliminius plicatus*). Several seaweed-grazing molluscs also abound, especially the ornate limpet (*Cellana ornate*), snakeskin chitons (*Sypharochiton pelliserpentis*) and the pupu or cat's eye (*Turbo smagardus*).

The tide pools are rich with life, especially a bewildering variety of seaweeds. Several seaweeds begin their lives in a flat and lichen-like form, before developing into coral-like tufts. A good example is *Corallina officinalis* which is bright red. Also common are the sheets of bright green sea lettuce (*Ulva lactuca*) and the rather unusual Neptune's necklace (*Hormosira banksii*), which looks like chains of beads. Red sea anemones (*Isanctinia tenebrosa*) are common, as are small fish such as the cockabullie or common triplefin (*Forsterygion lapillum*) and the small shrimp *Palaemon affinis*. Tidal pools are also the favoured home of whelks, *Cominella* spp. and several crabs, including the kaunga or hermit crab (*Pagarus novaezelandiae*) and the purple shore crab (*Leptograpsus variegatus*).

Other species to look out for, but which are found a little lower down in pools that are only accessible at low spring tides, are the edible paua or abalone (*Haliotis australis*) with the beautiful mother-of-pearl lining to its shell, and the spiny kina or sea urchin (*Evechinus chlororictus*). Both of these have suffered from over-fishing, as have some of the surf clams mentioned above. On more exposed rocky coasts you will find the massive bull kelp or rimurapa (*Durvillaea antarctica*), which can grow up to 20m long.

Pancake Rocks at Punakaiki on the west coast of South Island are fascinating examples of eroded limestone. JF

CLIFFS

Low rocky cliffs are quite common, especially on North Island, and these support a variety of plants, the most attractive and notable being the salt-loving, red-flowered pohutakawa (*Metrosideros excelsa*), with its often knarled and knotted trunk and boughs. It frequently leans down to the water's edge, hanging onto the cliff and also holding it together. Pohutakawas are found naturally only as far south as Taranaki and Poverty Bay, but have been planted much further south as an ornamental. Also common here are the New Zeland flax (*Phorium tenax*) with its spectacular flower spikes, much loved by tuis and bellbirds, and taupata (*Coprosma repens*) with its broad, shiny, dark green leaves and dangling flower stamens.

Okarito Lagoon. TDR

ESTUARIES AND COASTAL WETLANDS

Before the arrival of European settlers, New Zealand had extensive wetlands, often associated with estuaries. In many places large amounts of rock, sand and sediment have formed bars and spits, partly blocking river mouths and forming large wetland areas behind them. The estuaries are generally still there, but much of the wetlands surrounding them has been reclaimed for urban development or agriculture and only 10% of the original wetlands remain. The whole of Christchurch is built on land that was originally a swamp, but today there is just one tiny remnant. In the Bay of Plenty some 400km² of wetland have been drained to create land suitable for dairy farming, leaving just 1% for the wildlife.

There are some 300 estuaries in New Zealand. Many are quite small but some are very large, such as Kaipara Harbour in Northland, which covers over 150km². Estuaries and their associated wetlands are rich in wildlife, being at the interface of the land and the sea, and are prime areas for birdwatchers. Early Maoris relied heavily on estuaries for fish and shellfish, and they are still of value for this purpose. The waters of the estuary are rich in phytoplankton and zooplankton, food for fish, molluscs and smaller crustaceans, which in turn are food for birds, larger fish and larger crustaceans.

In the mud are a wide variety of mudworms and shellfish. The native cockle or tuangi (*Austrovenus stutchburyi*) is found in large numbers, as is piipi (*Paphies australis*), a mussel-like bivalve which, as well as being food for spoonbills, oystercatchers, sand flounders and other wildlife, is harvested for human consumption. There are three

Mangroves are widespread in the sheltered harbours of North Island. JF

common species of crab: the tunnelling mud crab or kairau (*Helice crassa*) lives in the upper tidal zone, while the stalk-eyed mud crab (*Macrophthalmus hirtipes*) is found in the mid and lower intertidal zone, and the hairy-handed crab or papaka huruhuru (*Hemigrapsus crenulatus*) is more generally spread – you may find it under rocks or detritus.

Many species of fish live in the estuaries, including two species of mullet, the grey (*Mugil cephalus*) and yellow-eyed (*Aldrichetta forsteri*). Other fish, such as the whitebait or inanga (*Galaxias* spp.), come down the rivers in the autumn to spawn in the estuaries. The young are then carried out to sea on the tide and return in the spring to ascend the rivers again, if they are lucky enough to escape the many nets put out by the numerous fishermen. New Zealand's whitebait season is a bit like the grouse season in the UK, but much more widely celebrated. In contrast, eels (*Anguilla* spp.) spend time in the estuaries as immatures before ascending the rivers. Other fish, such as snapper (*Pagrus auratus*), gurnard (*Lepidotrigla brachyoptera*) and red cod (*Pseudophycis bachus*), come into the estuaries to feed when immature and then return to the sea.

The grey mangrove (*Avicennia marina*), a tree which grows partly submerged in salt water, is widespread in sheltered estuaries and inlets in North Island, south as far as the Bay of Plenty. Ecologically speaking, it is an important tree, providing protection to the shore and wildlife, and the submerged parts of mangrove forests act as nurseries for young fish and other marine organisms. The trees grow to around 15m high in the far north, but are small and shrubby at the southern end of their range. They are becoming more numerous and widespread in New Zealand, partly because of the increased amount of silt brought down by the rivers – a phenomenon largely caused by human activities.

Wet grasslands and marshes surround many estuaries, with parts being regularly flooded at high water. Common native plants here include raupo or bulrush (*Typha angustifolia*) and harakeke or New Zealand flax. Both of these plants were important to early Maoris, who used them for building and food. The Maoris also used harakeke to make clothing, rope, fishing nets and lines, and even children's toys. The tall grass toetoe (*Cortaderia fulvida*), which is similar in appearance to the introduced pampas grass but with attractively drooping flower heads, is also common here, as is the rather odd-looking spiky-leaved cabbage tree (*Cordyline australis*) that is such a feature of lowland New Zealand. These plants were also much used by the Maoris.

With this wealth of life, it is little wonder that estuaries often abound with birds, especially waders, and not just the resident natives such as oystercatchers (*Haematopus* spp.), stilts (*Himantopus* spp.) and banded dotterel (*Charadrius bicinctus*), but huge numbers of migrants such as the bar-tailed godwit (*Limosa lapponica*) and lesser knot (*Calidris canutus*), which arrive in September and October and stay until late March or early April. Larger wading birds found include royal spoonbill (*Platalea regia*), white-faced heron (*Ardea novaehollandiae*) and occasionally the all-white kotuku or white heron (*Egretta alba*), along with native ducks such as Australasian shoveler (*Anas rhynchotis*) and grey teal (*Anas gracilis*), as well as red- and black-billed gulls and several species of tern.

The variable oystercatcher is one of the commonest coastal birds. JF

THE FORESTS

Before the arrival of man, around 80% of New Zealand was covered with forest, with North Island being almost completely forested. Over the 500 years following the arrival of the Polynesian settlers, around 75% of the dry forest in the east of South Island was destroyed by fires, almost certainly started by the settlers. Deforestation also occurred in the North but on a lesser scale. By the time European settlers arrived, around 1840, forests still covered around 75% of North Island and 50% of South Island.

The zeal and speed with which the Europeans destroyed the forests and their native fauna and flora – 80,000km² in not much more that 100 years – is a sad and familiar story. Today only some 20% of original forest cover remains, much of which is in fairly remote, mountainous and hard-to-access areas. Today the tide has turned and there are native bush regeneration projects throughout the country.

The forests fall into two basic types: mixed conifer-broadleaf and beech. The former can then be broken down by altitude into swamp, lowland and montane. However, there is considerable variation within these broad categories, with climate, soil, altitude and latitude all affecting each forest area's composition. Conifer-broadleaf forests are found throughout North Island and along the west and south coasts of South Island. Beech forests are more widespread in South Island, especially at higher elevation, but restricted to higher central areas on North Island. Unlike the beech trees of the northern hemisphere, New Zealand's beeches are evergreen.

EVERGREEN OR DECIDUOUS?

Almost all trees and shrubs in New Zealand are evergreen. Of hundreds of species, only about ten, including the kotukutuku or tree fuschia (*Fuschia excorticata*) are deciduous, while a further 17, including the wineberry (*Aristotelia serrata*) and kowhai (*Sophora macrophylla*) are semi-deciduous. Botanists originally thought that the reason for the predominance of evergreen trees was the relatively mild, sunny and moist climate, which enabled evergreens to photosynthesise throughout the winter. It is, however, not quite that simple, and while this is a factor, another is the relatively nutrient-poor soils that give the resource-hoarding evergreens the edge over deciduous trees, which are rather more profligate in throwing away their leaves every autumn.

CONIFER-BROADLEAF FOREST

Conifers are ancient plants that produce seed cones but not flowers, and generally have narrow or needle-shaped leaves. The 20 endemic species found in New Zealand belong to four families, the most widespread of which are the podocarps, which roughly translates as 'stalked fruit'. All are evergreen and grow throughout the country, but in the far south they are restricted to lowland areas. Broadleaf trees are large-leaved, usually evergreen (in New Zealand at least), flowering trees. Conifer-broadleaf forests, when fully developed, can be divided into five different layers:

- very tall emergent trees, mainly podocarps and other conifers, 30–50m tall
- a canopy of large broadleaf trees up to about 20m tall

- an understorey of smaller trees and tree ferns up to 15m tall
- shrubs and small or juvenile trees up to 3m tall
- the forest floor with ferns, grasses, mosses, liverworts and herbaceous plants

In addition, vines and epiphytes abound, the latter especially in wetter areas where trees can be almost completely hidden by these epiphyte 'gardens'.

SWAMP FOREST

A large percentage of swamp forest has been lost to agriculture and urban development. Where it remains, however, the dominant podocarp is kahikatea or white pine (*Dacrycarpus dacrydioides*), a tall, erect tree, often festooned with epiphytes and notable for its buttress roots. Such roots are also a feature of pukatea (*Laurelia novae-zealandia*), a flowering tree that uses pneumataphores – breathing roots – due to the waterlogged nature of the ground it grows in, as does the rather smaller swamp maire or maire tawaki (*Syzygium maire*).

Tasman National Park is one of the most accessible parks, with forest right down to the water's edge. TDR

LOWLAND AND COASTAL FOREST

New Zealand's lowland forest is a temperate rainforest with generally high rainfall and warm or mild temperatures. These conditions promote luxuriant growth, and forests are characterised by the large variety of species. In the far north the dominant is often kauri (*Agathis australis*), a truly impressive tree, one of the largest and longest-living in the world, with massive straight trunks that can have a girth of 16m or more and a height of up to 50m. The largest individual specimens, Tane Mahuta or 'Lord of the Forest' and Te Matua Ngahere, 'Father of the Forest', are reckoned to be nearly 2,000 years old. Both are in Waipoua Forest in the far north – see them if you can; it will be a memorable highlight of your trip.

The impressive kauri have incredibly straight, smooth, branchless trunks. TDR

The crowns of these massive trees are laden with nest epiphytes (*Astelia* spp.), members of the lily family. Young kauri, or 'rickers', often grow in small groves. Their leaves are larger and broader than those of adult trees. The bark of the kauri is unusual – it peels off in large rounded flakes, leaving reddish 'scars'. The same thing occurs in some other tree species; it is a mechanism for discouraging vines and epiphytes from growing on or climbing the trunk. Most kauri forest was heavily logged, so that only remnants remain in Northland and Coromandel.

Elsewhere, rimu (*Dacrydium cupressinum*) is the dominant podocarp in much northern lowland forest. This is a tall, quite narrow, very straight tree with graceful drooping leaves and branchlets. Older specimens, which can be 800–1,000 years old, are often festooned with epiphytes. Rimu may protrude 20m or more through the canopy and are clearly identifiable from above. However, when you are in the forest all you can see is the trunk, with its rough, flaking, almost shaggy-looking bark. Other podocarps here are matai or black pine (*Prumnopitys taxifolia*), which has a distinctive shrubby juvenile stage, miro or brown pine (*P. ferruginea*), and totara (*Podocarpus totara*), with its thick, stringy, deeply furrowed bark.

The only broadleaved trees to challenge the podocarps in height are the ratas (*Metrosideros* spp.). A rata starts its life as an epiphyte or occasionally a climber, and gradually envelops its host tree, often a rimu, remaining when the host dies. Most rata produce a profusion of crimson flowers, providing a flash of contrasting colour in an otherwise green forest.

The canopy in a typical lowland forest is made up of several broadleaved species, notably taraire (*Beilschmiedia taraire*), tawa (*B. tawa*), kamahi (*Weinmannia racemosa*) and hinau (*Elaeocarpus dentatus*). Beneath them is a sub-canopy of shrubs and smaller trees such as coprosmas (plants of the coffee family) and trees and shrubs of the genus *Pittosporum*, as well as the stately tree ferns. On the forest floor there is an amazing variety of ferns, some quite large and luxuriant, as well as mosses, lichens, liverworts and fungi.

On the coast the forest is often dominated by pohutakawa (*Metrosideros excelsa*) with its thick rough bark, broad spreading outline and dramatic outburst of brilliant fluffy red flowers in the spring and summer. Some have a profusion of aerial roots hanging down like curtains. Pohutakawa occurs naturally only on North Island but has been widely planted in streets, parks and gardens elsewhere. Puriri (*Vitex lucens*), which has crimson flowers and large red fruit, is another broad-spreading tree that often reaches a considerable age. Many small trees and shrubs form the understorey, including ngaio (*Myoporum laetum*), taupata (*Coprosma repens*) and karo (*Pittosporum crassifolia*).

MONTANE FOREST

The forest changes gradually with altitude: tree heights reduce as you climb higher up in the mountains. Most montane conifer-broadleaf forest is found on North Island and Stewart Island (on South Island beech forest predominates). Here kamahi is an important canopy tree along with kapuka (*Griselinia littoralis*). The conifers here are mountain or Hall's totara (*Podocarpus hallii*) and the rather conical mountain cedar (*Libdocedrus bidwillii*), along with the red-flowered northern or southern rata. Depending on the latitude, the montane forest blends gradually into sub-alpine scrublands.

Tree ferns are common components of the understorey in lowland forest. TDR

In Kahurangi National Park coastal forest climbs to high alpine fellfields and screes. TDR

SHRUB OR BABY TREE?

One interesting feature of New Zealand trees is that a number of them have a juvenile stage that is quite distinct from the mature tree. The commonest example of this is the lancewood (*Pseudopanax crassifolia*), which starts off as a single shoot with very long, thin, downward-pointing dark reddish-green leaves. From this it progresses into a trunk about 3–5m tall with a spherical mass of foliage on the top, the leaves still quite long and narrow but becoming more yellow-green. At maturity it is a medium-sized, very bushy tree, with green leaves. Another remarkable example is pokaka (*Elaeocarpus hookerianus*), which as a young tree is a confused mass of intertwined twigs and branches with very small leaves of varying shapes. It matures into a 12m-high canopy tree with small, oval leaves. The leafless bush-lawyer (*Rubus squarrosus*) starts off as a dense tangle of leafless stems with yellow hooks, and only develops leaves when it climbs into the canopy. Juvenile stages can last for as long as 60 years and enable the tree to survive long periods in the gloomy conditions of the forest undergrowth, waiting for a break in the canopy into which it can grow.

BEECH FOREST

In contrast to the wide range of species in podocarp-broadleaf forests, beech forest can be almost a monoculture, with few other species in the canopy, a sparse understorey and very few vines and epiphytes. This is partly due to the light-excluding nature of the beech canopy and the thick carpet of leaves that develops on the forest floor – the fallen leaves decay very slowly and so inhibit seed germination. There are four species of New Zealand beeches: red, black (which also has a mountain form), silver and hard. They belong to the genus *Nothofagus*, or 'false beech', and are found at higher altitudes and on poorer soils than the conifer-broadleaf forests. Beech forests are found predominately on South Island and do not occur at all on Stewart Island, or Mount Taranaki. This is thought to be because they spread very slowly and have not had time to penetrate that far south or west, since the last ice age, some 20,000 years ago.

In many mountainous areas, especially on South Island, beech forest is found right up to the 'tree line' – the upper altitude limit for trees. The closer you get to the tree line, the smaller and more stunted the trees become – they are often festooned with lichens and mosses, resulting in what is often called a 'goblin forest'. The tree line varies from about 1,500m in central North Island, down to 500m in the far south.

Of the four species of beech, the largest is the red beech (*Nothofagus fusca*), which grows to a height of 30m, while the mountain form of black beech (*N. solandri var. cliffortioides*) is the smallest at around 15m – sometimes less than a metre high close to the tree line. These two, along with the hard beech (*N. truncata*), develop buttress roots in mature trees. Many beech forests in South Island, especially those of black beech (*N. solandri var. solandri*), are infested by sooty beech scale insects (*Ultracoelostoma* spp.), which secrete honeydew, an important food for native insects and nectar-feeding birds such as the tui and bellbird. Introduced wasps (*Vespula* spp.) have taken a liking to this honeydew and consume a large proportion of it, with a damaging but unquantified impact on the native species.

Beech forest understorey is little more than ferns and mosses. TDR

LAKES AND RIVERS

Lakes and rivers form an important part of the ecology of the country and are a significant habitat for many species. From the alpine tarns and long glacial lakes of South Island to the large volcanic lakes of Taupo and the Rotorua area, they come in many forms. Taupo is New Zealand's largest lake at 612km². New Zealand has 300 or so rivers that reach the coast. As it is a long narrow country, its rivers are mostly quite short, with only ten that are more than 200km long. The longest, the Waikato, which flows north out of Lake Taupo, is just 425km long – less than a fifth that of Australia's longest river.

THE LAKES

The North Island lakes can be good for birds, though fishing and watersports in some tend to force the birdlife into quiet corners. Pollution is also a problem in some lakes, thanks to the increased human population and the run-off of chemicals from agricultural land, which affects populations of native and introduced fish. The lakes in Te Urawera National Park are less disturbed, and though fishing and boating are still allowed there, it is only during the holiday period when there are many people about. Hot springs and hot sand can provide ecological variations and Sulphur Point on Lake Rotorua is a notable birdwatching location. New Zealand scaup (*Aythya novaeseelandiae*) and Australasian shoveler are two of the ducks you're likely to see here. Native bush comes right to the shores of Rotoiti and Rotama, but this area is only really accessible by boat – try hiring a kayak.

The deep glacial lakes of the South Island have catchments that have been little modified by humans, due to their locations amongst mountain ranges. Local farming is at a lower intensity here than in other parts of the country; this, combined with low population density, has restricted nutrient input to the lakes, with most of them maintaining high water quality and clarity. These are the jewels among New Zealand's lakes, and they include the deepest lake in New Zealand, Lake Hauroko in Fiordland, with a maximum depth of 462m. These deep glacial lakes harbour increasingly rare native aquatic plant communities – although as they are largely below the water they're not easy to appreciate. While many are remote and difficult to access, the lakes can also be good for birds in summer and provide breeding grounds for some species.

THE RIVERS

The rivers in Northland, Bay of Plenty and Coromandel are short and often end in large harbours or estuaries. In Waikato they are longer, slower and have deeper and muddier beds and banks. Others further south have carved large gorges, especially through soft volcanic and sedimentary deposits. Many of these northland rivers are popular for watersports such as white-water rafting, kayaking and jet boating, which are not always compatible with seeing wildlife. Access is not easy on most of these rivers though you can reach interesting native bush via the Wanganui River and Gorge.

South Island, especially to the east of the Southern Alps, is well known for its spectacular braided rivers. These can be several kilometres wide with an amazing pattern of criss-crossing channels and shingle banks, formed as the river changes its course with the increased spring flow when heavy rains coincide with the melting snows. These wide riverbeds provide important habitats for a variety of native animals, especially birds, as well as plants. It is here that the wrybill (*Anarhynchus frontalis*), the only bird on earth with a bill that bends sideways, breeds in spring and summer. Terns, waders and gulls also favour braided rivers for breeding and with them come predatory species such as the New Zealand falcon (*Falco novaeseelandiae*) and the Australasian harrier (*Circus approximans*).

The Buller River flows out of Lake Rotoiti in the Nelson Lakes National Park. JF

ALPINE AND SUB-ALPINE

The alpine areas offer some of the most pristine habitat in New Zealand. They are extensive, covering some 30,000km² or 11% of the country. Most of this is in South Island along its mountainous spine. On North Island it is limited to the central volcanoes Tongariro, Ngauruhoe and Ruapehu, Mount Taranaki and the peaks of the mountain ridge running northeast from Wellington to East Cape. The alpine zone extends from the tree line up to the permanent snow line. In some areas alpine plants are found at much lower altitudes, such as Mount Moehau on the Coromandel Peninsula and on Stewart Island where they can even reach sea level. This is in part due to these plants being adapted to poor soils and adverse climatic conditions such as strong winds. On the offshore sub-Antarctic islands, Campbell, Auckland and Antipodes, the alpine zone extends to the coast. The snow line, where the alpine zone stops, is at approximately 2,000m.

The common feature of most alpine plants is that they are small and grow very low to the ground. This low stature is an adaptation to their short growing season and the low temperatures, high winds and heavy rainfall they must endure. There are obvious exceptions to this 'rule': herbaceous plants that die down in the winter, bulbs such as the bulbinellas, and the Mount Cook lily (*Ranunculus lyallii*), which is in fact the largest buttercup found anywhere. Various species of native speargrass or spaniard also send up tall spiny flower spikes. Often you need to get down on hands and knees to see a plant clearly and a lens of some sort can be helpful to really appreciate the small-scale beauty and variety of alpine plants. There are some 600 species of alpines, 20% of the New Zealand native flora, and the large majority are found nowhere else on earth.

Where beech forest predominates, the tree line is often dramatically evident, but in other areas there is a fairly gradual transition to what is generally termed sub-alpine shrubland. This area, which in some places is quite extensive, contains a

Alpine plants are adapted to cope with snow at any time. TDR

Vegetable sheep are common plants in the alpine areas of South Island. TDR

bewildering variety of low, very dense shrubs, with a great range of leaf shapes and colours. The resultant terrain can be difficult to traverse unless there is already a trail you can follow, so dense and ground-hugging is the vegetation. One attractive and distinctive shrub found here is the grass tree or dracophyllum (*Dracophyllum* spp.) with tufts of long, narrow, drooping leaves giving the plant a somewhat pineapple-like appearance. Also here are mountain cabbage trees (*Cussonia indivisa*), several species of tree or shrub daisy (*Olearia* spp.), and three species of dwarf or mountain conifers.

Within the alpine zone, above the tree line and the mountain shrublands, there are four basic habitat types: grassland, wetland, stable rock and rock debris or scree. Each of these has its own ecology. A number of factors or influences go towards forming these habitats, including altitude, rainfall, cloud cover, aspect, rock type, fertility and drainage.

GRASSLAND

The dominant plants in these alpine grasslands, which can be quite extensive, are snow tussocks of the genus *Chionochloa*. These are large, slow-growing and long-lived evergreen grasses, which may be several centuries old and often up to 2m in height, larger than many alpine shrubs. One of the most attractive and widespread of these is the red tussock (*C. rubra*), which is also the only one found in the north; it is also frequently used as an ornamental. The snow tussocks can dominate the scenery, with relatively few other plant species visible – those that you are most likely to see are the speargrasses or spaniards (*Aciphylla* spp.), members of the carrot family, with

47

Grasslands are important upland habitats for a number of invertebrate species. JF

their large, very spiny flower spikes, and the mountain buttercups (*Ranunculus* spp.) with their attractive large white flowers. Other plants sporting white flowers include the mountain foxgloves or ourisias (*Ourisia* spp.), gentians (*Gentiana* spp.) and several species of mountain daisy (*Celmisia* spp.). In some areas, shorter meadow-grass type grasses, which are also evergreen, predominate; here there is a much greater variety of other plant species.

WETLAND

The valley bottoms in alpine areas are often poorly drained, and bogs and wetlands are common, especially around small lakes or tarns. Mosses are common here, especially the peat-forming sphagnum mosses (*Sphagnum* spp.), along with a wide range of liverworts, sedges, rushes and lilies, especially the tall golden bulbinellas (*Bulbinella* spp.). You may also notice the carnivorous sundew plants (*Drosera* spp.), with their round or spoon-shaped hairy leaves on which unsuspecting insects get stuck and then digested by the plant. There are six native species of sundew and three are found in alpine areas.

STABLE ROCK

This habitat is characterised by rocky outcrops and thin soils. Here the plant life is varied and often very small and ground-hugging, especially some of the shrubs, which look like spreading herbs until you look closer. This is where the alpine flora is perhaps at its richest. Here you will find such botanical wonders as the woolly-looking vegetable sheep (*Raoulia* and *Haastia* spp.), and whipcord hebes which look more like clubmosses than shrubs. Daisies are also common, both herbaceous and shrub species. They are from several genera – *Celmisia*, *Brachyglottis*, *Helichysum* and *Cassinia* – and often have soft, downy leaves. Their daisy-like flowers or rounded fluffy seed heads will help you identify them. Other alpine shrubs found here include members of the hebe family as well as coprosmas, many of which have minute leaves. Also common here are lichens; New Zealand has a large selection with an array of striking colours and patterns.

Douglas Peak stands 3,077m at the head of the Fox Glacier. TDR

ROCK DEBRIS, SCREE AND FELLFIELD

This extreme habitat is largely restricted to the eastern slopes of the Southern Alps on South Island. At first glance scree slopes are not the most promising location for plants, but in spite of the constantly changing surface, a dozen species of small specialised plants live here, notably the penwiper plant (*Notothlaspi roulatum*) whose roots go deep into the sandy substrate beneath the mobile scree. If the scree surface moves, cutting off the flowering portion of the plant, it will sprout again from the rootstock.

Fellfield is a slightly more stable habitat than scree and is found above the alpine herbfields and just below the snow line. It is a harsh environment but surprisingly rich in plant life. Fellfield consists largely of loose rock with patches of thin soil, and is favoured by many cushion plants, such as mountain sheep and donatia, with their multitude of tiny rosettes often covered with surprisingly large flowers. In cracks and hollows a wide variety of diminutive plants take hold, including hebes, daisies, buttercups, gentians, sedges and grasses.

ALPINE ANIMAL LIFE

As with the plant life, so the animal life in the alpine region is highly specialised. Birds are quite scarce but the famous kea (*Nestor notabilis*), the world's only alpine parrot, is not uncommon and is notoriously inquisitive and destructive. Park your car in kea habitat at your peril, for these birds are enthusiastic vandals of automobiles, a particular favourite target being the rubber from around car windscreens. The smallest bird in the alpine region is the diminutive rock wren (*Xenicus gilviventris*), and New Zealand's only native falcon can also be seen here, often hunting the large alpine dragonflies that are common in late summer.

Two of the most surprising inhabitants of the alpine zone are the scree skink (*Oligosoma waimatense*) and the black-eyed or alpine gecko (*Hoplodactylus kahutare*). The geckos live in boulder piles and screes above 1,200m. They are nocturnal and have very variable colouring and patterns. Recent research indicates that there are actually several other species of alpine skink and gecko, most as yet undescribed, so if you see one try to photograph it or take notes – scientific glory awaits! The scree skink is found only on unstable screes in the east of the Southern Alps above 1,000m, where you may see one basking in the sun.

Invertebrates are well represented in the alpine region. Some, such as butterflies, moths, grasshoppers and dragonflies, are quite easy to observe, but you'll need to search out some others, such as the various species of weta and the numerous beetles. Another surprising find you may make here is the world's only alpine cicada. A very high proportion of all these alpine invertebrates, probably over 90%, are endemic. One of the big dangers facing them is global warming. Rising temperatures will force them higher up the slopes but they will soon run out of mountain – at present rates of decline many of these unique species could be gone by the end of the century.

BIRDS

Northern royal albatross chicks take nine months to fledge. TDR

When New Zealand broke loose from Gondwanaland 80 million years ago, the dinosaurs still ruled the world and mammals barely had a foothold. As a result, the birds that were on board at the time of the separation, or later made it across of their own accord, evolved into a diverse array of forms, most of them unique to New Zealand, to fill niches that are elsewhere filled by mammals. Everything changed with the arrival of earth's most destructive mammal – at least 41 species, nearly 50% of the country's native land bird species, have become extinct since man reached the islands.

If you've travelled halfway round the world from Europe, you may be disappointed by the homely flavour of the common birdlife, which includes European starling (*Sturnus vulgaris*), blackbird (*Turdus merula*), song thrush (*T. philomelos*), house sparrow (*Passer domesticus*), goldfinch (*Carduelis carduelis*), chaffinch (*Fringilla coelebs*) and yellowhammer (*Emberiza citrinella*). This is largely because the European settlers sought to convert the New Zealand bush to a European agricultural and urban environment, complete with familiar wildlife from home. The net result of these introductions, coupled with rampant habitat destruction, was a catastrophic decline in native bird numbers and the extinction of yet more species. Other non-natives thrown into the mix include the common myna (*Acridotheres tristis*) from Asia, and from Australia the Australian magpie (*Gymnorhina tibicen*) and the eastern and crimson rosellas (*Platycercus elegans* and *P. eximius*), two species of noisy, brightly coloured parakeets. Only recently have conservationists managed to reverse the decline of the native species, but there is a long way to go. To observe native species you need to find the native habitat. Apart from special protected areas, coastal wetlands, native bush and alpine areas are the best places to try.

The two notable features of native New Zealand birdlife are the high proportion of endemics (species unique to the country), and the number of flightless or near flightless birds. Nearly 20% of all native species are found or breed only in New Zealand and its offshore islands. Of the land birds, six are flightless, along with two species of duck found only on the sub-Antarctic islands. Many of the extinct species were also flightless.

The northern Buller's albatross is a frequent visitor to coastal waters. TDR

SEABIRDS

Perhaps it is not surprising in a country with such a length of coastline and quantity of islands that the large majority of New Zealand birds should be sea, coastal or wetland species. Over 75% of all native breeding species are seabirds or coastal and wetland birds and about a third of those – some 70 species – are members of the 'tubenose' group, so called for their distinctive tubular nostrils: the albatrosses, petrels and shearwaters. There are significant numbers of other species,

Salvin's albatrosses are frequently seen off the main islands, especially near Kaikoura. TDR

including penguins, shags, gulls and terns, as well as numerous migrant waders that breed in the Arctic and overwinter here during the southern summer.

TUBENOSES

Many of the tubenosed seabirds found in New Zealand are essentially oceanic, and either breed on offshore islands or don't breed locally at all but merely visit New Zealand waters on their wanderings. Therefore, unless you take a boat out to sea, you are unlikely to see many of them, though a few can be seen quite close inshore. These birds vary in size from the huge southern royal albatross (*Diomedea epomophora*) with its 3.5m wingspan and 11kg bulk, to the diminutive grey-backed storm-petrel (*Oceanites nereis*), which is just 18cm long and weighs a mere 35g.

While almost all of these species are spring and summer breeders, the three large albatross species have an 11-month breeding cycle, while two others, the Westland petrel (*Procellaria westlandica*) and the common diving petrel (*Pelicanoides urinatrix*), are winter breeders. Apart from the albatrosses, all the other tubenoses breed in burrows, mainly on offshore islands, but sometimes high up in the mountains of the Coromandel, Kaikoura or Westland. Most only visit their colonies at night, to avoid the attentions of predators.

Albatrosses

Few experiences in the bird world compare to an encounter with a large albatross. Icon of the open sea and immortalised in mariners' legends since man first took to the ocean, the effortlessly gliding albatross is the living embodiment of a truly global freedom. New Zealand is albatross capital of the world, with ten species breeding here, eight of which breed nowhere else. Most species breed on the remote sub-Antarctic islands, to the south and east of the main islands. There is, however, a small colony of northern royal albatrosses (*Diomedea sanfordi*) on Taiaroa Head near Dunedin. This species and the southern royal albatross are huge black-and-white seabirds with wingspans of up to 3.5m and massive flesh-coloured bills. They are extremely long-lived and travel vast distances, especially when not breeding. Newly fledged birds have rather brown plumage but become whiter as they grow older. Mature males are the whitest of all albatrosses. The other large albatross breeding

Chatham albatrosses have the smallest breeding area of any bird species. TDR

here that you may see is the Antipodean albatross (*D. antipodensis*), one of the four species of wandering albatross. This is slightly smaller than the royals, and much browner, often having a chocolate-brown head and body and a white face, giving it a hooded appearance.

Six species of mollymawk, rather smaller albatrosses with only a 2m wingspan, also breed in New Zealand. All are white-bodied with almost black upperwings, and are identified mainly by their head and bill colouring. Two have white heads: the white-capped albatross (*Thalassarche steadi*), which has a dull greyish yellow bill, and the Campbell albatross (*T. impavida*), with a bright yellow-orange bill. The other four are grey-headed: Salvin's albatross (*T. salvini*) which has a mainly dull grey bill, Chatham albatross (*T. eremita*) which has a deep yellow bill, and Buller's (*T. bulleri*) and grey-headed albatrosses (*T. chrysostoma*), both of which have black bills with bright yellow upper and lower ridges.You are unlikely to see the smoky-grey light-mantled albatross (*Phoebetria palpebrata*) unless you venture well south.

You can see albatrosses anywhere around the coast. Some particularly good places are the crossing at Cook Straight or Foveaux Straight, off Kaikoura on the east coast of South Island, and in the Bay of Plenty; you can take boat trips to see them in these places. You may also see the black-browed albatross (*Thalassarche mealnophyrs*) that breeds in the Falklands; it is very similar to the Campbell but has dark rather than golden eyes.

New Zealand breeding albatross species, breeding locations and status

Great albatross

Antipodean	Antipodes Islands, Campbell Islands	Endangered
Northern royal	Taiaroa Head, Chatham Islands	Endangered
Southern royal	Campbell Islands, Auckland Islands	Endangered

Mollymawks

Campbell	Campbell Islands,	Endangered
White-capped	Auckland Islands, Antipodes Islands	Endangered
Chatham	Chatham Islands,	Endangered
Buller's	Chatham Islands Snares Islands, Solander Islands Three Kings Islands	Endangered
Grey-headed	Campbell Islands	Near-threatened
Salvin's	Bounty Islands	Endangered
Light-mantled	Campbell Islands, Antipodes Islands	Near-threatened

Large dark shearwaters and petrels

Whether you're on a boat or watching the sea from the shore, you're likely to notice these graceful birds shearing low over the waves. Perhaps less graceful than some is the northern giant petrel or 'stinker' (*Macronectes halli*), which is about the size of a small albatross. It is a well-known scavenger with a massive horn-coloured bill. The sooty shearwater or titi (*Puffinus griseus*) is rather smaller, with narrower wings, and is much more numerous. It is nicknamed 'mutton bird', and its young are still collected for food in some areas. There are several other all-dark 'tubenoses', commonest of which are the flesh-footed shearwater (*P. carneipes*), and three petrels: the white-chinned petrel or 'shoemaker' (*Procellaria aequinoctialis*), the Westland petrel (*P. westlandica*) and the grey-faced petrel (*Pterodroma macroptera*). This last is browner than the other three with a greyish face, while the white-chinned is just that and the Westland is all-dark.

The stinker or northern giant petrel has a powerful bill. TDR

The white-chinned petrel nests on sub-Antarctic islands to the south. TDR

Medium-sized petrels

There are a number of slightly smaller petrels, the most striking of which is the cape pigeon or pintado petrel (*Daption capense*), with its attractive black-and-white pattern on the upperwing; pintado means 'painted' in Spanish. Several other species have a distinctive dark 'W' pattern on their pale-grey upperwings – this helps camouflage the bird against the waves and thus avoid the attention of winged predators. The commonest medium-sized tubenose in New Zealand is Buller's shearwater (*Puffinus bulleri*), which breeds on the Poor Knights Islands off Northland; it is most frequently seen in the late summer and autumn when it disperses from the breeding grounds. Prions have wide bills, equipped inside with narrow plates called lamellae that work like combs, enabling the birds to sieve plankton out of mouthfuls of seawater. The fairy prion (*Pachyptila turtur*) and the broad-billed prion (*P. vittata*) have similar plumage, and the latter is particularly well endowed on the bill front. The mottled petrel (*Pterodroma inexpectata*) and the black winged petrel (*P. nigripennis*), have similar plumage patterns to the prions, but additionally have distinctive black markings on the underside of the wing.

Pintado petrels or cape pigeons are commonly seen offshore. TDR

Small petrels

Smaller tubenoses include fluttering shearwater (*Puffinus gavia*), Hutton's shearwater (*P. huttoni*) and little shearwater (*P. assimilis*). These are all white-bodied with dark or black upperwings. They frequently feed in large flocks, often quite close inshore and have fast wingbeats and an amazing ability to 'fly' underwater, reaching depths of 5m or more. Smallest of all is the common diving petrel, a very small, dumpy black and white petrel which seems to spend much of its time underwater. Diving petrels also often feed in flocks and if disturbed will suddenly appear on the surface and take off – but seem to have to work very hard just to stay airborne.

The white-faced storm-petrel is a graceful and attractive surface feeder. JF

Storm-petrels

If you notice a sparrow-sized bird gliding or fluttering along low over the sea, you're probably looking at a storm-petrel. The name 'petrel' is derived from St Peter, who, according to legend, walked on water, and these little seabirds appear to do the same thing, flying with their long, delicate legs dangling down to touch the water's surface. Six species have been recorded in New Zealand waters, but the two you are most likely to see are the grey-backed and the white-faced (*Pelagodroma marina*), the former having an all-dark head, the latter a white chin and broad white eye stripe.

PENGUINS

You may think of penguins as denizens of the Antarctic wastes. If so, it may come as a surprise that six species breed in New Zealand, while another seven regularly visit New Zealand waters. The species you are most likely to encounter on the main islands is the little blue penguin (*Eudyptula minor*). This dumpy little bird is the smallest penguin in the world, at just 40cm long and just over 1kg in weight. It is mid-blue-grey above, white below with a dark bill, and breeds all around the coast including the Bay of Islands, Tiritiri Matangi Island, Banks Peninsula and Wellington Harbour. In some places you'll notice road signs for 'penguin crossings', warning drivers to watch out for tiny,

The little blue penguin is widespread around the coast. TDR

Yellow-eyed penguins come ashore in the late afternoon. TDR

waddling pedestrians. Distinctly larger is the yellow-eyed penguin (*Megadyptes antipodes*), which has typical black-and-white penguin markings but a yellowish head and a bright yellow band from eye to eye round the back of the head. You are most likely to see this bird on South Island, from Dunedin round to Fiordland, and on Stewart Island. Of a similar size is the Fiordland crested penguin (*Eudyptes pachyrhynchus*), which is like the yellow-eyed but has a black head with distinctive frowning yellow eyebrow plumes and a stout dark orange bill. It is quite rare but may be seen in Fiordland and on Stewart Island. The other three penguins breeding in New Zealand also possess tufty yellow eyebrows of varying degrees of extravagance: the Snares crested penguins (*E. robustus*), erect-crested penguin (*E. sclateri*) and the rockhopper penguin (*E. chrysocome*) are all normally found only in the sub-Antarctic islands.

SHAGS AND CORMORANTS

These elegant, long-necked and long-tailed diving seabirds are commonly seen around the coast or on inland lakes. There are 12 species in New Zealand, eight of which are endemic and the other five nearly so. They are surface divers, propelling themselves along underwater with their broad webbed feet in pursuit of fish. When hunting they spend much of the time underwater, surfacing only briefly for air. When on the surface their long bodies sit very low in the water. All species breed in the spring and summer apart from the black shag (*Phalacrocorax carbo*) and spotted shag (*P. punctatus*), which are year-round breeders. Six species are common or locally common.

The largest is the black shag or kawau, a bird with a global distribution – you may know it from Europe as the cormorant or great cormorant. It is blackish-brown all over with yellow facial skin at the base of the bill and a white patch on the cheek and chin. In breeding plumage it develops white feathers on the crown and neck as well

Spotted shags may breed at any time of year. TDR

The little shag is easily recognised by its size and short bill. TDR

The Australasian gannet is very similar to its northern counterpart. TDR

as a white thigh patch. The little black shag or kawaupaka (*P. sulcirostris*) is also all dark but with a greenish sheen. It is much smaller and has no white markings, and is found only in North Island and the northern end of South Island.

The other shags are all essentially black and white. Largest is the pied shag or karuhiruhi (*P. varius*), a mainly coastal bird found mostly in northern North Island and northwest, northeast and southwest South Island. It is basically black above and white below, with a dark line running down the flank to the leg. The bill is pink, eye ring blue and there is a yellow patch at the base of the bill. The smallest is the little shag (*P. melanoleucos*) which is widespread and found more frequently on inland waters, harbours and estuaries. It has a short yellow bill and two plumage phases. In the pied phase it is similar to the pied shag but without the dark line on the flank; in the white-throated phase it is all-dark apart from a white throat and face. The spotted shag or parekareka (*Stictocarbo punctatus*) is slightly smaller than the pied shag and has a brown back, grey breast and yellow feet; in breeding plumage it develops a white stripe down the neck and a tufty double crest. It is commoner in South Island than in North. The Stewart Island shag (*P. chalconotus*) is found there and on the southeast coast of South Island; it is much smaller than the pied shag but with similar plumage, pink legs and pink at the base of the bill. It also has a dark bronze plumage phase.

The king shag (*P. carunculatus*) is similar to the pied but found only in the Marlborough Sounds, while the five other endemic black-and-white shag species are found on the offshore islands of Campbell, Auckland, Bounty, Chatham and Pitt Island in the Chatham Islands. The Pitt Island shag (*P. featherstoni*) is similar to the spotted shag, while the others are similar to the Stewart Island shag and are best identified by location – should you be fortunate enough to get there.

BOOBIES AND TROPICAL SEABIRDS

Named after the Spanish word *bobo* or clown, boobies are graceful plunge-divers and elegant on the wing – the unflattering name relates to their rather clown-like behaviour, especially when courting. Only one species is commonly seen off the main islands and that is the Australasian gannet (*Morus serrator*), a large black-and-white seabird with a very handsome creamy-yellow head and an impressive dagger-like bill. It is widespread and breeds at several locations around the coast, especially on North Island. There are large, accessible colonies at Cape Kidnappers in Hawkes Bay, Muriwai near Auckland and Farewell Spit in Golden Bay. Two other species of boobies may be seen in New Zealand waters. The masked booby (*Sula dactylatra*) breeds on the Kermadec Islands. It is similar to the Australasian gannet but smaller with a white head and yellow bill. The brown booby (*Sula leucogaster*) is a rare vagrant.

Two species of tropicbird and two frigatebirds are known from New Zealand waters. However, only the red-tailed tropicbird (*Phaeton rubricauda*) – a glorious white plunge-diving seabird with a bright red bill and very long red central tail feathers – breeds here (and only in the Kermadecs). The others are occasional vagrants.

SKUAS, GULLS AND TERNS

While there are more than 25 species of skuas, gulls and terns on the New Zealand bird list, most of these are confined to the sub-Antarctic islands (skuas) or the tropical Kermadec Islands (terns and noddies).

Skuas

These powerful opportunists are the original pirates, hounding and robbing other seabirds of their catches and killing smaller birds when they get the chance. The brown skua (*Catharacta skua*) is a large, heavily built, aggressive predator and scavenger with dark brown plumage, which breeds on Stewart Island as well as the Chathams and sub-Antarctic islands. You may notice brown skuas lurking ominously around colonies of nesting seabirds, waiting for their chance to attack any unattended chick or egg. This is the species you are most likely to see on the mainland, though the rather more aerodynamic and longer-tailed arctic skua (*Stercorarius parasiticus*) is also frequently recorded at sea, often quite close inshore. Arctic skuas breed in the northern hemisphere, but travel widely across the world's oceans when they're not busy with parenting duties.

Be sure to wear a hat whenever you are near nesting brown skuas. TDR

Red-billed gulls quickly show up at a picnic. TDR

Gulls

There are only three species of gull in New Zealand; all are relaxed in human company and take advantage of any food available. The largest is the southern black-backed or kelp gull (*Larus dominicanus*), a very effective scavenger found across the southern hemisphere. It breeds around the coast of all three main islands and the offshore islands. It is a distinctive large white-bodied gull with black upperwings and a yellow bill. If you see a similarly sized brown gull, that will be a juvenile; southern black-backs take up to four years to reach adult plumage. They are found inland as well as on the coast.

The red-billed gull (*L. novaehollandiae*) is much smaller and more numerous. It has a white body, grey upper wings and bright red legs, feet and bill, and is found all round the coast. It will soon come and introduce itself to you if you decide to have a picnic by the sea. It is very much a bird of the coast and coastal wetlands, though it is also found in the volcanic lakes of central North Island. The only endemic member of the family is the black-billed gull (*L. bulleri*). Slightly smaller than the red-billed, it is paler, has a black bill and dark, slightly reddish legs and feet. Like the southern black-back, it is found inland as well as on the coast, but is more scattered and prefers South Island.

The white-fronted tern is the commonest species around the coast. TDR

Terns

This group of elegant, raucous seabirds has 18 New Zealand representatives, of which one, the black-fronted tern (*Sterna albostriata*), is endemic. In breeding plumage the black-fronted tern is a handsome bird with a rather grey body, jet-black cap and bright red legs, feet and bill; it loses its black cap in the non-breeding season. It is found mainly inland and on the east coast of South Island. The New Zealand fairy tern (*S. nereis davisae*) is an endemic subspecies which, sadly, is critically endangered. Like many terns, this dainty bird nests on beaches and so is very vulnerable to ground predators, disturbance by people and extreme weather conditions. It breeds only in Kaipara Harbour north of Auckland and on the east coast opposite. The commonest terns are the Caspian tern (*S. caspia*), a hefty, short-tailed tern with a huge red dagger of a bill, and the white-fronted tern (*S. striata*) which is largely white with grey upperwing, black cap, nape, bill, legs and feet. Both are largely coastal terns with the former found on some larger inland lakes. They are found all around both islands but especially from the Hauraki Gulf northwards. The white-fronted is found in much greater numbers than the Caspian which is generally in pairs or small groups. The other species are either tropical terns found only in the Kermadec Islands or occasional visitors.

WATERSIDE AND WETLAND BIRDS

Because so much of pre-human New Zealand was forest and mountains, wetlands were very important open areas for wildlife. Before the arrival of European settlers there were large areas of wetland, but most of these have been drained to provide additional farmland and only 10% of the original wetlands remain today. As an example, in 1890 the coastal wetlands in the Bay of Plenty covered 40km², but less than 1% of that remains today. Fortunately it is less easy to modify harbours and estuaries (though pollution is a problem here) and work is in progress to reclaim and expand wetland areas across the country. There are significantly more waterside and wetland birds than there are land birds, so this is where you are most likely to see native species.

WADERS

With its lengthy coastline and large sheltered estuaries and harbours, together with broad inland braided rivers, New Zealand is a wader paradise with some 60 species recorded. Approximately half of these are regular migrants from the northern hemisphere, flying thousands of miles to spend the southern summer in New Zealand. The rest are either resident natives, or vagrants and stragglers, especially from Australia.

The pied oystercatcher is easily recognisable by its massive orange bill. TDR

Large native waders

Of the natives, the most widespread are probably the oystercatchers (*Haematopus* spp.). These large black or black-and-white birds with long pink legs and a long, strong orange bill are found all around the coast. The pied oystercatcher or torea has a black head, neck, wings and back-and-white undersides. The variable oystercatcher is slightly larger and has two phases, an all-black one and a black-and-white one which is very similar to the pied, but with a rather more diffuse boundary between the black neck and white belly. Oystercatchers are very much birds of the coasts and harbours, feeding on a wide variety of shellfish as well as crabs and invertebrates (although not usually oysters).

The other common black-and-white wader is the delicate pied stilt or poaka (*Himantopus himantopus*). This bird has

The pied stilt occurs inland as well as on the coast. TDR

61

extremely long, thin, bright pink legs and a long thin bill, and is more widely distributed, being found inland, often on small farm ponds, as well as on the coast. Its all-black cousin, the critically endangered black stilt or kaki (*H. novaezelandiae*), is extremely rare and breeds only in two locations in central South Island, but wanders further afield, to coastal harbours and estuaries, including Manukau and Kaipara in the winter. Another large wader that is also found inland as well as on the coast is the spur-winged plover (*Vanellus miles*), which can often be identified by its noisy behaviour: its call is a loud staccato scream. Failing that, its black cap, yellow bill and facial mask together with its tumbling irregular flight should help you identify it. Note that this is a different bird from the spur-winged plover of the northern hemisphere. Spur-wings are a relatively recent arrival to New Zealand, having first bred here in 1932. They are now everywhere, beneficiaries of the large areas of open farmland.

The bent bill of the wrybill is unique. AM/NSI

Small native waders

Smaller native waders are represented by three species of dotterel, the very rare shore plover (*Thinornis novaeselandiae*) and the wrybill (*Amarhyncus frontalis*) with its uniquely bent beak. A dapper little plover with a black necklace, the wrybill breeds in the braided rivers of central South Island and disperses during the winter, especially to northern North Island. Manukau and Kaipara harbours and the Firth of Thames are good places to see this unusual bird out of season. No-one is quite sure why the bill bends to the right, but it does appear to help the wrybill feed on invertebrates underneath stones, enabling it to reach further underneath a stone without having to turn it over.

Dotterels have a rather upright posture and a characteristic behaviour pattern. If you approach them on the beach they run away very fast two or three times and then take off, often flying back to where they started. Two of the three native species of dotterel are endemic. The more widespread is the banded dotterel or tuturiwhatu (*Chadrius bicinctus*), which is readily identifiable from the endangered New Zealand dotterel (*C. obscurus*) by its dark collar and broad rufous breast-band. The banded dotterel (see page 181) is a coastal breeder on North Island, but breeds inland too on South Island. The New Zealand dotterel lives mainly in the northern half of North Island where it is a beach breeder, and on Stewart Island where it breeds on the sub-alpine tops. It is generally more approachable than the other two. The third species is the black-fronted dotterel (*Charadrius melanops*). Smallest of the three, it has a prominent black eyestripe and heavy black chest-band, yellow legs and a black-tipped red bill. It breeds mainly along the southeast coast of North Island and the

Bar-tailed godwits migrate to New Zealand from their breeding grounds in the Arctic. NF

east coast of South Island. The very rare endemic shore plover was until recently confined to the Chatham Islands, but has been introduced to North Island where it breeds on the Mahia Peninsula in Hawkes Bay. It is very small, quite short-legged and can be identified by is broad black head-band and black-tipped red bill.

Large migrant waders

New Zealand is the holiday destination of choice for a large number of waders that breed in the Arctic. They come to the country dressed in their drab winter plumage, so provide you with the perfect opportunity to hone your wader identification skills.

The bar-tailed godwit (*Limosa lapponica*) is probably the most numerous winter visitor, with well over 100,000 birds arriving between late September or early November. Its arrivals and departures are much celebrated in New Zealand literature. Some of the birds you see will have touched down fresh from a non-stop eight-day flight of 11,000km from Alaska, the longest known single non-stop journey made by any bird. Others arrive a little later after taking a somewhat longer route with some stop-offs, via Asia and Australia. The 'barwit', as it is nicknamed by birdwatchers, is a sturdy bird with a very long, slightly upturned bill, dark legs, a pale throat and belly and a barred tail that is only visible in flight. The fact that it forms large flocks, sometimes as many as 10,000, is a useful identifying feature. This species is most numerous in North Island, especially in the Firth of Thames and in Tauranga, Manukau and Kaipara harbours. It is less numerous in South Island, as there are fewer suitable estuaries and harbours there. Most birds leave for Alaska in March or April with anything up to 18,000 birds remaining here over winter, mainly immatures. If you examine the flocks carefully, you may find a few Hudsonian godwits (*L. haemastica*) and black-tailed godwits (*L. limosa*) feeding with the bar-tails. They are best distinguished in flight as both have striking black tails and white rumps, while the black-tailed has a straight rather than upturned bill.

The only migrant waders larger than the godwits are the eastern curlew (*Numenius madagascariensis*) and the whimbrel (*N. phaeopus*). Both are large long-legged brown waders with long downcurved bills. The curlew is the larger of the two and has a much longer bill, while the whimbrel has dark stripes above its eyes. Both birds' calls are distinct and evocative, the curlew having the haunting 'cur…leeeew' while the whimbrel has a clear seven-note call.

Small migrant waders

The small shorebirds that patter about close to the water's edge may look drab at first, but take a closer look and you'll appreciate their subtle patterns and endearing characters. Commonest of the smaller migrant waders is the lesser knot or huahou (*Calidris canutus*), with large flocks of up to 10,000 birds congregating in the Firth of Thames, and in Tauranga, Manukau and Kaipara harbours as well as Farewell Spit and Nelson Bay in South Island. The lesser knot breeds in Siberia and arrives in New Zealand in September and October. It is a rotund, solid-looking bird with pale grey-brown plumage, and a rather short, pointed, black bill; and a tendency to go about in very large flocks. The great knot (*C. tenuirostris*) in winter plumage is very similar but is slightly larger and stockier, with a much longer bill.

There are a number of migrant sandpipers, commonest of which are the curlew sandpiper (*C. ferrugea*), a pale tawny wader with a long downcurved bill and faint pale eyebrows, and the sharp-tailed sandpiper (*C. acuminata*) which has a more upright posture, brighter rufous plumage and a rather short, slightly downcurved bill. The smallest migrant waders are the stints, which have dark legs and shorter bills than the knots or sandpipers. The commonest of these is the red-necked stint (*C. ruficollis*) which in flight shows a white rump with a dark centre, and a white wing-bar.

Similar in size to the two knots is the Pacific golden plover (*Pluvialis fulva*), an upright, alert-looking wader with a short black bill and largely brown plumage with slightly chestnut wings, a pale belly and grey legs. It is found mainly on North Island, especially from Firth of Thames northwards. The one migrant wader you'll easily identify by its plumage is the turnstone (*Arenaria interpres*), also known as the ruddy turnstone. This dumpy, approachable wader has strikingly variegated chestnut, black and white breeding plumage and short orange legs, a distinct black chest-band and a short, very slightly upturned bill. Should you see a wader swimming on the sea, this will be one of the phalaropes (*Phalaropus* spp.). All of the world's three species of phalarope occur in New Zealand but all are very rare.

GREBES

Grebes are not well represented in New Zealand, despite the country's wealth of lakes and other wetlands – ideal habitat for these elegant freshwater fish-eaters. There are just three native species, one of which is endemic and one an occasional visitor from Australia. The endemic species is the New Zealand dabchick (*Poliocephauls rufopectus*), a small, squat waterbird with a long, distinctly reddish neck. Dabchicks make prolonged and frequent hunting dives. Like other grebes they indulge in a lovely formalised courtship ritual, reminiscent of an aquatic square dance. They are found in lakes and ponds throughout North Island with occasional records from South Island. Much larger is the Australasian crested grebe (*Podiceps cristatus australis*), the Antipodean subspecies of the great crested grebe you may know from home. This bird lives on inland lakes on South Island, often gathering on coastal lakes in the winter. It is mid-brown with a long neck and long dagger-like bill, a distinctive chestnut ruff and a dark crest. The third native species, the Australasian little grebe (*Tachybaptus novaehollaniae*), is smaller than the dabchick and lives mainly from Auckland northwards. In breeding plumage it has a black head with a distinctive chestnut-brown patch on the neck and a yellow mark at the base of the bill.

DUCKS, GEESE AND SWANS

You may be surprised to learn that New Zealand, despite its many lakes and historically extensive wetlands, has few waterfowl: just eight native ducks, no native geese, and one recently arrived native swan. However, a further four ducks, two geese, a swan and a coot have all become extinct since the arrival of man. Many of the surviving ducks are rare and with very restricted ranges. Of the eight native species only four are likely to be seen anywhere besides out-of-the-way places or on special reserves such as Tiritri Matangi Island or Tawharanui.

Ducks

You should not have to wait too long for your first encounter with the handsome paradise shelduck or putangitangi (*Tadorna variegata*). Found almost everywhere, this species is unusual among wildfowl in that the female is more brightly coloured than the male. She is bright chestnut with a white head and neck and black-and-white wings, while the male has a rather dark grey body, black head with a deep green gloss, and black-and-white wings. Paradise shelducks are found in coastal marshes and inland wetlands, but have also adapted well to open farmland where they breed on small ponds. You will nearly always see them in pairs – they are quite noisy, especially during courtship when they have long conversations, with the male often standing upright on a prominent log or mound. Sadly, they are still viewed as game birds and hunters shoot large numbers each year. The rather less brightly coloured chestnut-breasted shelduck (*T. tadornoides*) is very rare and found in scattered, mainly inland locations on both islands.

You have a reasonable chance of seeing four other species of native duck. The grey duck or parera (*Anas superciliosa*) occurs throughout the country and looks rather like a dark female mallard (*Anas platyrhynchos*), with which it will hybridise, but with a green rather than blue panel on the

The paradise shelduck is unusual in that the female has the more eye-catching plumage. TDR

wing. Its head pattern of dark crown, white eyebrow and heavy dark eyestripe gives it a supercilious look. The species has recently declined due to the loss of habitat, preferring lakes and rivers surrounded by forest rather than farmland, and also due to continued hunting. Rather less common is the Australasian shoveler (*Anas rhynchotis*). Larger than the grey duck, this bird has a very long, broad, spoon-shaped

The grey teal is common in coastal lagoons and inland lakes. TDR

The New Zealand scaup is the only dark, dumpy, diving duck. TDR

bill, and while the female is rather inconspicuously brown, the male in breeding plumage is a colourful bird with a dark grey head, white 'tear-drop' markings, a boldly scalloped breast and chestnut flanks. Shovelers prefer lakes to rivers and live throughout the country, but hunting has an inevitable impact on numbers. Smaller and less widespread than both the shoveler and the grey duck is the grey teal (*A. gracilis*). This slight, rather upright duck has a pale throat and cheeks and a large green wing-bar in flight, but is otherwise a rather unremarkable pale grey flecked with brown. It is found from the far north to Southland, but is absent from the mountains, Westland and Fiordland. The New Zealand scaup (*Aythya novaeseelandiae*) is a small, dark, diving duck. The male's head has a dark green sheen, against which his bright golden eyes stand out clearly, while the female is dark-eyed with uniformly mid-brown plumage. Scaup are found in some harbours and estuaries but you are most likely to encounter them on inland lakes; as with other species they are more widespread out of the breeding season.

Two uncommon endemic ducks are the blue duck or whio (*Hymenolaimus malocorhynchos*) and the brown teal or pateke (*Anas aucklandica*). The blue duck inhabits fast-flowing streams and rivers, in forest and tussock country. Conservationists are reintroducing captive-bred birds in several locations and so you now have a better chance of seeing it. The brown teal has a very restricted distribution, though you can see it on Tiritiri Matangi Island and other reserves. It is closely related to two similar but flightless species, Auckland Island teal and Campbell Island teal (*A. aucklandica* and *A. nesiotis*).

There are a number of Australian ducks that occur from time to time, but the only introduced species is the mallard, which makes up for the lack of other aliens by being the most numerous duck in the country. In fact there are probably more mallards in New Zealand than there are individuals of all the other duck species put together. This is largely because it has adapted well to the new urban and agricultural habitat.

The black swan has dramatic white outer wings, visible only in flight. TDR

Geese

There are no surviving native geese in New Zealand. The commonest goose is the ubiquitous Canada goose (*Branta canadensis*) with its unmistakable black, white and brown colouration. It was first released in 1876, but did not become established until further introductions in 1905 and 1920. It is now found throughout the country apart from Stewart Island and has become a pest species in some areas. The Cape Barren goose (*Cereopsis novaehollandiae*), an odd-looking all-grey Australian species, has become established in scattered locations, especially near Christchurch and Auckland. Escapee or feral farmyard geese (*Anser anser*) are widespread in North Island and the eastern half of South Island.

Swans

The black swan (*Cygnus atratus*) is the only common swan in New Zealand. It was introduced in 1864, but ornithologists believe that wild birds arrived from Australia under their own steam at about the same time. Black swans are now widespread on larger lakes and ponds and nest in large numbers on North and South islands, so much so that in some areas they have become pest species for the damage they can cause to pastures. The all-white mute swan (*C. olor*) is another introduced species, but it has been less successful and survives at only a few scattered locations.

HUNTING AND FISHING

Hunting and fishing in New Zealand are national passions on a par with rugby or adventure sports. Many of the original settlers came here to escape a structured, class-oriented society where hunting and fishing were the leisure pursuits of the wealthy. In New Zealand, which is in some ways still a frontier society, almost anyone may be involved in one or more of these activities, especially fishing. Hunters and fishers contribute an important political voice that has a big impact on conservation policy and action, not always positive. Hunters, for instance, are keen to have large areas of protected native bush to hunt in, but do not want all the deer, pigs and goats eradicated as there would be nothing left to hunt! Fishermen are not always happy with marine reserves, even though they have been shown to help fish stocks. Trout, introduced as a sports fish, is known to affect the populations of native freshwater fish.

The game bird hunting season generally runs from early May to the end of July or August, but it varies depending on species and location. There are clear rules regarding bag size, type of pellets, boats and hides. It is unfortunate that while there are a large number of alien game birds available to hunt, several native species, including grey duck, pukeko, shoveler and paradise shelduck, are also hunted. Hunting introduced game birds makes sense, hunting natives does not.

SWAMPHENS, COOTS AND RAILS

This diverse group of birds is well represented in the country, with eight native species. Three of these rank among the most interesting and charismatic birds in New Zealand.

Takahe (*Porphyrio manteli*)

This is the biggest and most enigmatic of the three, a very large, heavy (3kg), deep blue, flightless bird with very sturdy legs and a massive triangular red bill. You are

The takahe's bill looks fearsome, but is used mainly for grazing grass and herbs. TDR

extremely unlikely to see one in the wild as they are restricted to a remote area of Fiordland, and indeed were at one point thought to be extinct, another victim of alien introductions. However in 1948 a small colony was located and since then captive and island breeding programmes have been developed. Thanks to these efforts, there are now around 300 individuals alive in the world today, although only about 30% of them are in the wild at present. Several sanctuaries, including Tiritiri Matangi and Kapiti, now have small breeding populations.

Pukeko
(Porpohyrio porphyrio melanotus)
In contrast to the takahe, the pukeko is a common and widespread bird in spite of being hunted during the season. It is a subspecies of the purple swamphen, which lives throughout Europe, Asia and Africa. The pukeko has adapted well to agricultural developments and can be seen in most lowland and grassland habitats throughout the country, apart from the very dry areas of South Island. It is a large, handsome dark blue-black bird. Its long, slim orange-red legs are equipped with similarly lengthy toes. Its bill and the frontal shield on its forehead are bright red and it has white

The pukeko is widespread and thrives in agricultural areas. TDR

underwings and undertail. Unlike the takahe, the pukeko has retained the power of flight – just! It can therefore perch and roost in trees, safe from the dreaded introduced mammalian predators. Pukekos have a distinctly comic appearance as they walk along with rather exaggerated, dainty steps, a trait even more pronounced in the young ones whose small bodies take a while to catch up with their oversized legs and feet. They are group breeders, each group consisting of two or more breeding females, a similar number of males and some non-breeders – often sub-adult birds from previous broods. Several females may lay their eggs together in any one nest and everyone in the group helps with feeding and caring for the chicks.

Weka *(Gallirallus australis)*
Wekas, like takahes, are flightless, but have not suffered quite such catastrophic declines, perhaps because of their bolshy and opportunistic natures. Even so, they disappeared from most of North Island 70–80 years ago, thanks to the usual combination of habitat loss and alien mammalian predation, and are now found only around Opotiki in the eastern Bay of Plenty and in a few island and inland sanctuaries. In South Island they are still retreating but are found largely in the north and west and in Fiordland. A subspecies (*G. a. scotti*) is found on Stewart Island, especially on Ulva Island in Patterson Inlet. Wekas here are easily seen,

Wekas, being flightless, have suffered a lot from invasive mammalian predators. TDR

especially on the beaches. They are quite aggressive, brown, chicken-sized birds with
sharp, powerfull bills. In a number of places they are very habituated to people, and
will approach you if they think you might have food.

Coots and rails

The country formerly had its own endemic coot, but this now resides on the
depressingly long list of extinct New Zealand birds. If you observe an all-black
waterbird with a white bill and frontal shield, then this is an Australian coot (*Fulica
atra australis*), not a common bird here but one that you may see on certain lakes such
as Rotorua and Rotoiti in central North Island. A weed-eater, it ranges from
Auckland to Southland in small lakes or near the shore on larger ones.

Three species of smaller rail are locally common. The banded rail (*Rallus
phillipensis*) is the largest and is found in the north of North Island, with a few in
northern South island. It is smaller than the weka with a brown back, grey and white
banded breast and white eyebrows. The spotless crake (*Porzana tabuensis*) is quite
small and dark and is largely confined to scattered locations throughout North
Island, more in the north than the south. The marsh crake (*P. pusilla*) is the smallest,
with barring on the wings and undertail. It has a very scattered distribution, with no
obvious regional pattern.

HERONS, EGRETS AND SPOONBILLS

These large, long-legged birds mostly make their living wading after small aquatic
creatures in shallow fresh water. Only one of the five species of native heron is
common – the white-faced heron (*Ardea novaehollandiae*), a rather slim grey heron
with a white face and chin and a slightly rufous breast. It lives throughout the
country in virtually all habitats but shows a clear preference for wetlands. The bird
is a relatively recent natural arrival from Australia, having first been reported in
1865. The other species, however, have smaller ranges thanks to habitat loss and
now climate change. Five species of all-white heron have been recorded but only the

white heron or kotuku (*Egretta alba*) breeds here. This is a globally distributed species and another recent arrival; the first known breeding took place in 1941 and it is now found scattered throughout the country in rough pasture and by lakes and estuaries. A very large all-white heron with dark legs and a large yellow bill, you are unlikely to mistake it for any other species. The other often observed white heron is the cattle egret (*Bubulcus ibis*), another worldwide species that has been expanding its range in all directions for decades. It does not breed in New Zealand (yet…) but Australian birds winter here. The reef heron (*Egretta sacra*) comes in two plumages, a rare all-white one and the much commoner all-dark one. It prefers rocky or mangrove coasts, hence its preference for the north of North Island, but it is also found in several areas in South Island including Fiordland, and also on Stewart Island.

Royal spoonbills have truly enormous flattened bills. TDR

A large long-legged white bird that you might at first glance mistake for a heron is the royal spoonbill (*Platalea regia*). With your second glance you will note the massive, very broad spoon-shaped black bill. It is found in coastal wetlands and estuaries, largely but not exclusively in the west of North Island and the north, east and south of South Island in coastal wetlands, and occasionally around Lake Taupo. Feeding spoonbills sweep their slightly opened bill from side to side, trapping any disturbed prey in it. The yellow-billed spoonbill (*P. flavipes*) is an occasional visitor from Australia.

Another large, long-legged waterside bird that you may be fortunate enough to spot, or at least hear, is the Australasian bittern (*Botaurus poiciloptilus*). While widespread, especially in northern North Island, this reed-loving bird is reluctant to show itself but its deep, breathy 'booming' call during the breeding season, from September to February, is very distinctive. If you should chance on a large heron-like bird with a long downcurved bill, this will be an ibis. Two species are occasionally seen: the all-dark glossy ibis (*Plegadis falcinella*) and the largely white Australian white ibis (*Threskiornis molucca*).

The white-faced heron is the commonest heron in New Zealand. JF

Brown kiwis have amazingly long bills and very stout legs. TDR

LAND BIRDS

Given that at least 80% of the country was once covered by fairly dense bush or forest, it is not surprising that most of the land birds that survived or evolved in New Zealand were adapted to life in the forest. When humans arrived, it was the land birds that suffered most. They were used as a ready source of food, and were very susceptible to predation by the rats. Between the arrival of the first Polynesians and the first Europeans, some 32 bird species became extinct, and nine more followed after the Europeans arrived – most of them land birds. The last to go, and hopefully the last for a long time, was the diminutive, almost flightless bush wren (*Xenicus longipes*) which disappeared as recently as 1972. These are the survivors.

KIWIS (*Apteryx* spp.)

Every visitor to New Zealand will want to see kiwis, and New Zealanders themselves are happy to be their namesakes. Certainly the most iconic of all surviving New Zealand creatures, kiwis have hung on despite the destructive impact of human activity, and today humans are striving to help them recover their numbers. These flightless birds, with their hair-like feathers, impressive sense of smell and nocturnal habits, provide a particularly good example of the 'birds doing the work of mammals' theme that is so typical of New Zealand, being ecologically more akin to ground-foraging mammals such as hedgehogs or bandicoots than to other birds. They are certainly most unlike their nearest relatives: the ostrich, emu and other members of the ratite family.

Females are generally larger than males, especially when about to lay – the egg is extremely large relative to the bird, weighing some 15–20% of her body weight. Though perhaps not much fun for the female kiwi, laying such a big egg means the chick within can safely develop to a high level of maturity – this strategy is, of course, impossible for birds reliant on flight. Males do most or all of the incubation of the single egg, and the chick wanders off and fends for itself a few hours after hatching.

Kiwis are nocturnal, and so not easy to observe in the wild. They were originally widespread and very numerous, but only remnant populations survive today, with much effort being put into habitat restoration, predator control and captive breeding. The use of offshore islands and specialist incubation facilities for their recovery is particularly significant and numbers are gradually increasing.

There were originally thought to be three species – brown, great spotted and little spotted – but at the turn of the century researchers carried out genetic tests on South and North island's populations of the brown kiwi, and as a result it was split into three distinct species. The North Island brown kiwi (*Apteryx manteli*) is found in a number of locations on North Island. The Okarito brown kiwi or rowi (*A. rowi*) is found near Okarito in Westland, and the Haast brown kiwi or tokoeka (*A. australis*) lives in Fiordland as far north as Haast and also on Stewart Island. The great spotted kiwi or roroa (*A. haastii*) is found in the northern half of South Island and the little spotted kiwi or kiwi-pukupuku (*A. owenii*) occurs in just a few locations in North Island and in the Marlborough Sounds. A number of kiwis are held in special reserves or sanctuaries such as Tiritiri Matangi, Kapiti, Bushy Park near Wanganui, Karori Sanctuary in Wellington and Otanewainuku in the Bay of Pleanty.

The largest kiwi is the great spotted (see page 10) – a female may weigh over 3kg. It is an almost spherical, flightless bird with an impressive downcurved bill, up to 15cm long, with which it forages for its main food: soil invertebrates. The sensitive nostrils are close to the tip of the bill, a feature not found in any other bird species. Around the base of the bill are a number of stiff or rictal hairs, which are thought to be of significance when foraging. It has large, long-toed feet and very strong stout legs.

The three brown kiwi species are slightly smaller than the great spotted, while the little spotted is much smaller at less than 1.4kg.

THE MOAS

Few species convey the unique nature of New Zealand birdlife in the way that the kiwis and moas do. Before man's arrival, the big, flightless moas were successful and widespread in New Zealand, filling the role that large grazing and browsing mammals like deer, cows and antelopes do elsewhere. That they had their own specialist predator in the fearsome Haast's eagle is another sign that their populations were healthy. There are thought to have been 11 different species of moa, ranging from the giant moa (*Dinornis giganteus*) that stood 3m tall and weighed an amazing 240kg, to the equally heavy but much squatter heavy-footed moa (*Pachyornis elephantopus*) and the smallest, the upland moa (*Megalapteryx didinus*) which stood a mere 1.3m high and weighed around 30kg. Moa eggs were equally large with the largest weighing up to 4kg and the smallest 500g. The gizzard of one sub-fossil moa contained 5.6kg of stones.

Moas were largely browsers and preferred trees and shrubs to grass; many native grasses are of the tussock or sedge type which are not very palatable. It has been suggested that it was the browsing of the moas that helped produce the remarkable divaricating trees and shrubs that are so common in New Zealand.

The New Zealand falcon is largely a forest bird. TDR

HAWKS AND FALCONS

The Australasian harrier or kahu (*Circus approximans*) is one of the most commonly seen native land birds. It is a large, brown bird with a long, square-ended tail, that cruises over open countryside with its wings held upwards in a distinct 'V' shape. Being both a predator and a scavenger, you may see it feeding on road kill or hunting over wetlands or scrublands. It is one of the few native species to have benefited from the clearance of the native bush. Australasian harriers are found throughout the country except in alpine and densely forested areas. The adults, especially males, are quite a pale brown, while juveniles are quite dark.

The other widespread raptor is the endemic New Zealand falcon (*Falco novaeseelandiae*), which is much smaller, with long, pointed wings and agile flight – it feeds mainly on smaller birds and large insects caught in flight. It is much less frequently seen than the harrier as it is largely a bird of the forest and upland areas. The only other raptors you may see in New Zealand are very rare visitors from Australia. The very dark black falcon (*F. subniger*) is significantly larger than the native falcon, while the Nankeen kestrel (*F. cenchroides*) has narrow straighter wings and typical kestrel hovering behaviour. The black kite (*Milvus migrans*) is occasionally seen and, while superficially similar in appearance to the Australasian harrier, it does not hold its wings upwards in a 'V' and it has a shallow fork in its tail.

OWLS

The onomatopoeically named morepork or ruru (*Ninox novaeseelandiae*) is New Zealand's only native owl. It is a small, dark brown, forest owl with glowing yellow eyes and a very distinctive call of 'more pork, more pork'. While widespread it is not found in open agricultural areas. Keep an eye out for this owl on forest tramps: it often sits motionless on top of dead trees or tree fern trunks. The other resident owl is the introduced little owl (*Athene noctua*). You are more likely to see this owl, which is smaller, paler and streakier than the morepork, in daytime and in open areas. An occasional visitor from Australia is the barn owl (*Tyto alba*). Larger and much paler than the other two, it can appear ghostly white in car headlights.

The morepork is more often heard than seen. TDR

KINGFISHERS

The New Zealand kingfisher or kotare (*Halcyon sancta*) is another species that has benefited from forest clearance and adapted to the agricultural landscape. It is a small, quite stocky bird with a very large, slightly boat-shaped bill. Look out for it perched on power lines, posts or solitary trees overlooking mudflats or pasture. Its plumage is blue-green above and pale buff below with a white collar, and it feeds on small fish, crabs, invertebrates and even lizards and small birds. New Zealand kingfishers occur throughout the country, especially in North Island, but are somewhat less common on South Island, especially in higher and drier areas. Should you see a much larger, brown kingfisher-like bird, this is probably a kookaburra – an Australian species that has been introduced to the north of North Island.

PARROTS AND PARAKEETS

New Zealand may not have the tracts of steamy rainforest that we associate with shrieking flocks of colourful parrots, but when you consider that Australia has over 50 species, New Zealand's seven native species start to seem like a meagre haul. Besides the natives, there are also five species introduced from Australia.

Kakapo (*Strigops habroptilus*)

This large nocturnal parrot is a record-breaker in more ways than one: it is the heaviest parrot in the world, at over 900g, the only flightless one; and possibly the longest-living bird on earth, with an average lifespan of around 90 years. It is also a bird of unique charm and character, with its soft, green plumage, owl-like face, 'jogging' gait and gentle nature. Like all the flightless birds the kakapo found itself ill-adapted to the sudden arrival of a host of ground predators, and very nearly became extinct. At the time of writing in 2008 there are 93 living individuals –

The kakapo is the world's only flightless parrot. TDR

precarious indeed, but actually a distinct improvement on the population of just 51 in 1995. Numbers have been boosted by an intensive recovery programme, but it is a slow process as kakapos are very slow breeders: in the wild they only breed every three to five years. Breeding in the wild is linked almost entirely to a good supply of food during the eight-month cycle. Success is also dependent upon a lack of predators, as the incubation, brooding and feeding is done entirely by the female. Kakapo are 'lek breeders'. Each male digs out a bowl-shaped depression with tracks leading to it; he then sits down in the bowl, inflates a special air sac in his chest and emits deep booming noises, which attract the females. The female inspects the bowls and listens to the males, then chooses her mate, mates with him and goes off to nest and bring up the young, while the male continues booming to attract further females. Kakapos now live only on pest-free offshore islands or in specialist breeding facilities.

A good view of a kaka will reveal its beautiful plumage. TDR

Kaka and kea

Two other endemic parrots that are locally quite common are the kea (*Nestor notabilis*) and the kaka (*N. meridionalis*). The kaka, a forest parrot, is the more widespread, with distinct subspecies on the two main islands. The northern subspecies is restricted to remote heavily forested areas such as the Te Urawera National Park Pureora Forest Park, and offshore islands. The southern form is found only in the north and west and on Stewart Island. Its plumage is olive green above and reddish below. The southern subspecies is more brightly coloured than the northern, and the males of both sub-species have rather longer curves to their bills than the females.

The kea, inhabitant of the alpine region, is a handsome bronze-green and olive green parrot with an extremely long downcurved upper mandible. It is

Keas are highly inquisitive – and often very destructive. TDR

very adept at using this to attack parked cars and is particularly good at removing the rubber seal around windscreens. On a more sinister note, it also uses this impressive weapon to extract shearwater chicks from their burrows and butcher them. Found only in upland areas of South Island, its clear, ringing, often echoing call of 'keee... aaa' is instantly recognisable. Until 1970 there was a bounty on keas as they were thought to attack live sheep. They do indeed eat dead and dying sheep, but although there is some evidence to suggest that certain individual birds may attack live sheep, they are not considered a significant threat. They are now fully protected.

Parakeets

There are five much smaller parakeets, all endemic but none of them easy to find. Two of them, the Antipodes parakeet (*Cyanoramphus unicolor*) and the Chatham Island parakeet (*C. forbsi*) are found only on their respective island groups. Malherbe's parakeet (*C. malhebi*) is critically endangered with a population of under 100 and found only in two valleys in central South Island. The most numerous and widespread species is the yellow-fronted parakeet (*C. auriceps*), an attractive bright green bird with a red-and-yellow forehead, which is found mainly in central North Island and in alpine areas on South Island and on Stewart Island. Rather more restricted is the red-crowned parakeet (*C. novaezelandiae*), which has a red crown, eyestripe and patch on the flank. Most red-crowned parakeets live on Stewart Island and offshore islands in the Hauraki Gulf such as Tiritiri Matangi. All of the native parakeets are seriously threatened by alien predators, particularly rats and stoats.

The red-crowned parakeet is especially fond of budding flowers. TDR

Introduced parrots and parakeets

Four parrots have been introduced from Australia. You are likely to see some or all of them, as they are all eye-catching birds and tend to live close to urban conurbations. The white sulphur-crested cockatoo (*Cacatua galerita*) is unmistakable, as is the smaller pink and grey galah (*C. roseicapilla*). Even more easily identified is the outrageously coloured eastern rosella, with its yellow, green and scarlet plumage, and the equally flashy crimson rosella, the female of which is at least partly clothed in modest green while the male is a vision of bright red and blue.

The kereru has a liking for flower buds and soft fruit. MJ

PIGEONS

The kereru (*Hemiphaga novaeseelandiae*) is the only native pigeon in New Zealand, a large, handsome but rather clumsy bird, bigger than the European woodpigeon which it superficially resembles. It has a dark blue-green head and neck, red bill and eye ring, a dark purplish-green back and tail, and white underparts. A bird of the forest, it is found in most lowland areas apart from the agricultural ones. It has a particular liking for the fruit of the rewarewa and puriri trees, whose fruits were also consumed by Maori – the kereru is therefore often found close to old Maori 'Pa' sites. There are two introduced species, the cosmopolitan and familiar rock dove or feral pigeon (*Columba livia*), which is widespread, and the sandy-coloured Barbary dove (*Streptopelia roseogrisea*), which is found very locally in North Island.

SWALLOWS, SWIFTS AND MARTINS

New Zealand has just one breeding swallow, the charmingly named welcome swallow (*Hirundo tahitica*), which is a typically graceful representative of its group. It is dark blue-grey above and white or pale below with a rufous face and throat and a deeply forked tail. This is another recent arrival from Australia, having been first recorded as breeding here in 1958. Welcome swallows are widespread throughout the country apart from alpine and high densely forested areas. They are probably partially migratory, heading north in the winter, but most appear to remain – though there is a movement away from higher and colder areas in winter. Two martins, the Australian tree martin (*H. nigricans*) and the fairy martin (*H. ariel*) are occasional visitors; both are greyer than the swallow and lack the deeply forked tail, while the fairy martin distinguished by its rufous-brown head. Two swifts, the spine-tailed swift (*Hirundapus caudacutus*) and the fork-tailed swift (*Apus pacificus*), also appear occasionally; the former has greenish upperwings, a white throat and undertail and a square tail while the latter is browner with a distinctly forked tail.

CUCKOOS

Both of New Zealand's native cuckoos are parasitic breeders, like their European counterparts. They are shy and difficult to see, both are migratory and are only around in very small numbers in North Island in the winter, returning in numbers in September. Both are forest birds and tend to skulk, so while you may hear them calling, you may only catch a brief glimpse as they dart from one tree or bush to the next. The smaller of the two, the shining cuckoo or pipiwharauroa (*Chrysococcyx lucidus*), is an attractive bronze-green on the back and wings with a white face, while the throat and undersides are barred with dark green. Its voice is a series of distinctive bi-syllabic *'coo-eee's*, with an upward lilt. Shining cuckoos are widespread but rather scattered, especially on South Island, and are not found in the main agricultural areas. They usually use the grey warbler as a foster parent for their offspring. The much larger long-tailed cuckoo (*Eudynamys taitensis*) is strikingly barred chestnut and black on the back and wings with a pale breast heavily streaked with brown and black. Its very long tail is diagnostic and its call is a rather harsh shriek. Long-tailed cuckoos generally choose whiteheads, brown creepers and yellowheads to look after their young.

There are four other cuckoos that occasionally visit: the pallid cuckoo (*Cuculus pallidus*) and Oriental cuckoo (*C. saturatus*) are generally grey, the former with white barring on the tail and undertail, while the latter has a barred breast as well. It also has a brown phase. The fan-tailed cuckoo (*Cacomantis flabelliformis*) is small, grey with a buff breast and barred tail while the channel-billed cuckoo (*Scythrops novaehollandiae*) is very much larger than any of the others with a very large bill, grey head, red eye patch and dark back and tail.

NATIVE SONGBIRDS

There are fewer than 20 native passerine (songbird) species left. Many of these have very restricted ranges and some are confined to sanctuaries. Being small they are the most susceptible to predation by rats, mice and stoats, and are also vulnerable to habitat loss.

Kokako (*Calleas cinerea*)

The largest of the native passerines is the kokako, a shy all-grey bird with a short, curved, heavy black bill and distinctive blue wattles on either side of its throat. It is a bird of the forest canopy and is not easy to see, even when you know it is there. You are most likely to find it by its wonderful call, a series of loud, mournful, sometimes whistling notes, rather like a tenor recorder, best heard at dawn. Kokakos used to be widespread, but

The kokako makes up for its rather dull plumage with its haunting song. MJ

the South Island subspecies *C. c. cinerea* has not been positively identified for more than 30 years and was declared extinct by DOC in 2004. Despite this, hope still remains, as calls and possible sightings are reported from time to time, so the search goes on. The North Island subspecies *C. c. wilsoni* is still found in the wild but is restricted to just a few areas of dense native bush in Bay of Plenty, the Te Urawera National Park and Pureora Forest Park. It is also on several island sanctuaries and will soon be in at least one inland island sanctuary.

Tui (*Posthamadera novaeseelandiae*)

One of the commonest of the endemic passerines, the tui (pronounced *too-ee*) is found throughout the country, but being a nectar feeder it is largely absent from agricultural regions as they don't have the native, nectar-producing trees and plants it needs. Looking rather like a large blackbird, it has a long, pointed, slightly down-curved bill, adapted for nectar feeding. Adults have a small white 'bow-tie' on their throat, which inspired its common English name 'parson bird'. In the breeding season the male's plumage is a wonderful glossy blue and green with delicate strand-like white 'filo-feathers' on the neck. The song of the tui is extraordinary: a diverse series of cackles, gurgles, wheezes and whistles, produced apparently with great effort. The composition varies from individual to individual, season to season and region to region. A notch in the primary wing feathers can also make the wing tips vibrate, producing a loud whirring noise in flight. Tuis are vigorous defenders of both their feeding and breeding territories. When not chasing off competitors they have a distinctive undulating flight. Tuis manage to survive in some urban areas as long as there are sufficient native plant species. Christchurch, being notable for its lack of native vegetation, has no tuis. The presence of cats, rats and possums is probably another factor.

The breeding plumage of the male tui is as unusual as its song. MJ

Bellbird or korimako
(*Anthornis melanura*)

The bellbird is another common and quite widespread species and, like the kokako, more often heard than seen. It is an olive green colour with darker wings and tail. Another nectar-feeder, it too has a fine down-curved bill, and is confined to native bush areas. Interestingly it is absent from most of North Island north of Hamilton, apart from the Coromandel and the offshore islands. In contrast it is well represented on Stewart Island. Its call is quite variable but is basically a series of clear, liquid bell-like notes, sung in any order. While not endangered, its numbers have been severely reduced by alien predators.

Bellbirds love the nectar in the New Zealand flax. TDR

Saddleback or tieke
(*Philesturnus carunculatus*)

Like the kokako, the saddleback has been severely affected by alien mammalian predators and is now found in just a few sanctuaries and offshore islands. A mainly black bird with a long, thin, very pointed bill, and a small red wattle on either side of base of the bill, it has a bright chestnut band across the back and wings, giving it its English common name, and a similarly coloured rump. There are different subspecies on North and South islands, but both are very similar in adult plumage. Saddlebacks often feed on the forest floor and have a piercing '*chi-te-te-te*' call.

The saddleback is particularly vulnerable to alien predators. TDR

New Zealand pipit or pihoihoi (*Anthus novaeseelandiae*)

The New Zealand pipit, like other pipits, is a classic 'little brown bird', rather non-descript pale brown with a streaked breast and distinctive white eyebrows. It is a bird of open country from the coast to alpine areas and is widespread – though is not very common anywhere. It avoids agricultural areas.

EXTINCT BIRD SPECIES

It is hard to believe that since the arrival of man, 41 species of endemic bird have become extinct in New Zealand. Perhaps even more surprising is the fact that 32 of these happened in the 500 years between the first arrival of Polynesian settlers and the first Europeans. As discussed, habitat clearance and the arrival of the kiore were the main culprits. Predation by humans could also have been significant – the moas in particular were an important food source for the first settlers, as would have been the eggs of most birds. An additional factor that may have had an impact is climate change. The last ice age peaked 20,000 years ago, and since then the climate has been warming, resulting in the spread of forest cover and reduction in open grassland habitat. This may have adversely affected populations of species adapted to the open habitats.

The 32 species that disappeared during this period were quite varied. They were 11 moas, four ducks, three each of rails and birds of prey, two each of geese and wrens, and a pelican, a swan, a coot, an adzebill (a very hefty rail-like bird), a snipe, a crow and an owlet nightjar. Many of these were either flightless or poor fliers and all almost certainly had little or no fear of man. The extinction of the colossal Haast's eagle *Harpagornis moorei*, the heaviest flying bird ever known, was probably a direct result of the extinction of the moas, its primary food source.

The arrival of European settlers, especially from 1840 onwards, heralded a new onslaught on native species, and nine additional endemic bird species have been lost in less than 200 years. The same main causes are there, but aggravated by improved technology and a wave of new alien mammalian predators. These last nine victims were two tiny wrens, a duck, a rail, an owl, a warbler, the piopio – which was related to the Australian bowerbirds – and the remarkable huia, a relative of the kokako and saddleback. The huia was the only bird ever known to show sexual differences in bill shape. Females had long , slender downcurved bills up to 10cm long, while the males had shorter, stouter bills up to just 6cm long. Huia tail feathers were black with a white band and were much prized by Maori, and later by Europeans. The last known wild pair were shot by a collector.

Common small songbirds

You are unlikely to observe more than five of the small native songbirds generally at large in New Zealand. To see the others you will probably have to visit an island or inland sanctuary, as most have been seriously affected by alien mammal predators. It is unclear why the three commonest ones have survived as well as they have.

One species that you are quite likely to see on a bush walk is the New Zealand robin (*Petroica australis*), a small, upright, dark grey-black bird with a small white spot at the base of its bill. It has a pale yellowish breast and belly, which is more prominent in the South Island subspecies *P. a. australis*, also known as the kakariwai. The robin is a perky, inquisitive bird and will often approach quite closely, especially if you sit down and are patient. The North Island subspecies *P. a. longipes* is found mainly in the central area from Bay of Plenty to Taranaki, while the South Island form is concentrated in the northwest and southwest. There is a separate subspecies on Stewart Island, *P. a. rakiura*, which has a slightly sharper dividing line between the dark and pale plumage on the breast.

Another bird you may see on a bush walk is the tomtit (*Petroica macrocephala*). There are two subspecies: ngiru-ngiru (*P. m. macrocephala*) in South Island and miromiro (*P. m. toitoi*) on North Island, with two further subspecies in the Chatham Islands and Auckland Islands. The North Island tomtit is a very small bird. The male is black with a white breast and belly, a broad white wing-bar and, like the robin, a small white patch at the base of the upper mandible. The female is brown rather than black, with a buff-coloured throat and upper breast. The South Island tomtit is very similar but the white underneath turns pale yellow and then orange where it meets the black of the throat. Tomtits are widely distributed, but being forest birds they avoid the main agricultural and urban areas. Look out for them searching for invertebrates in the foliage, or flying down to the ground and then back to a tree branch. They are rather less inquisitive than the robins.

The silvereye or tauhou (*Zosterops lateralis*) crossed over from Australia in around 1856 and has spread rapidly across the country. It is now found nearly everywhere, apart from the driest and highest areas. Although it is basically a nectar-feeder it is willing to tackle invertebrates and fruit as well – this versatility enables it to survive in most parts of the country. It is a small olive green bird with a prominent white eye ring that often travels in small flocks and is a regular visitor to bird tables, especially for sugar water. Its Maori name means 'stranger' indicating that the Maori noted its arrival.

One of the most delightful small native birds, the fantail or piwakawaka (*Rhipidura fuliginosa*) has also adapted to human presence quite well. It has two plumage phases – pied and black – and three sub-species: *R. f. placabilis* in the North, *R. f. fuliginosa* in the South and *R. f. penitus* in the Chatham Islands. The black or melanistic phase birds are found mainly in South Island and were originally thought to be a separate species – no-one has yet unravelled the significance of this form or why it should occur only in South Island. The pied phase birds have grey heads, brown backs and buff bellies, with black-and-white throat-bands and white eyebrows; the melanistic phase is grey-black all over. The fantail's most distinctive feature is its very long tail with black central and white outer feathers, which it fans out in flight as it 'bounces' or flits around catching insects. Fantails will often approach you in the bush, perhaps hoping you may disturb insects which they can eat. They are found almost everywhere, especially on North Island, other than very high and very dry areas.

The most widespread endemic songbird in New Zealand is the grey warbler or riroriro (*Gerygone igata*). You may see it anywhere, apart from the highest tussock grasslands. A small,

Silvereyes are frequently seen feeding on flax flowers. TDR

top Fantails often accompany you on walks in the bush. MJ
middle The South Island robin will often approach quite close if you sit quietly. TDR
bottom The tomtit is very much a bird of the forest. TDR

rather inconspicuous insectivorous bird, it is grey above and paler underneath with pale eyebrows. Often seen searching diligently through foliage for insects, it is the unwitting nest host for the shining cuckoo. The closely related Chatham Island warbler (*G. albofrontata*) is slightly larger and has a rather more prominent eyebrow.

Uncommon small songbirds

The populations of these species have suffered serious declines for the usual reasons. Some are found only or mainly in island or inland sanctuaries.

The most endangered of these small passerines is the stitchbird or hihi (*Notiomystis cincta*). Only ever a North Island species, it is now confined to island sanctuaries, with the biggest population on Little Barrier Island. Stitchbirds are rather noisy, their piercing whistle-like call quite ear-splitting if given in concert. The male has a black head, neck, upper breast and back with a distinctive gold-orange border; the rest of the body is brown, but it has a white mark behind the eye. The female is brown with a white wing-bar. Slightly more widespread but equally endangered is the tiny rock wren or matuitui (*Xenicus gilviventris*), which is confined to the alpine and sub-alpine regions of South Island. A perky little bird with rather long legs and virtually no tail, it is a reluctant flyer. It is a slightly olive green above with a pale belly, yellow flanks and a white eyebrow. Even smaller, at only 8cm in length and weighing just 6–7g, is the rifleman or titipounamu (*Acanthisitta chloris*). The male is bright yellow-green above and pale below with a white eyebrow and a very sharp upwardly curved beak. The female is streaky brown with the same white eyebrow. This tiny bird is found in upland and sub-alpine forest, especially beech and tawa. It often travels in parties, and older people may be unable to hear its very high-pitched call. There are two distinct subspecies, *A. c. chloris* in the south and *A. c. granti* in the north.

The fernbird (*Bowdleria punctata*) is another species with separate subspecies on the two main islands, and two more on Stewart and Codfish islands. A small brown secretive bird with a very long tail, it is more often heard than seen. It has a distinctive metallic '*oo-tchk*' call, and a pair will often 'talk' to each other. It prefers rushes and scrub vegetation by wetlands and is widespread but scattered. Three

Hihis can make an amazing amount of noise when together. TDR

other endemic passerines have more restricted ranges. The smallest is the brown creeper or pipipi (*Mohoua novaeseelandiae*), not to be confused with the North American bird of the same name, a small brown bird with a grey nape which is found only on South Island – mainly on the flanks of the alpine cordillera. It is the main host of the parasitic long-tailed cuckoo in South Island. The yellowhead or mohoua (*M. ochrocephala*) is another foster-parent for the long-tailed cuckoo. It is larger, with a yellow head and breast, and has a more restricted range, being found mainly in the far southwest on South Island. The closely related whitehead or popokatea (*M. albicilla*), also a cuckoo foster-parent at times, is found only on North Island, in a band from Bay of Plenty to Taranaki and further south near Wellington.

BLACK ROBIN

Probably the most famous individual bird to have lived in New Zealand is a female Chatham Island black robin (*Petroica traversi*) known as 'Old Blue'. This remarkable bird was the last fertile female of her species in 1980, with only three males surviving with her on Little Mangere Island in the Chathams. The birds were moved to Mangere Island, which had more untouched habitat, and a recovery programme got under way. Thanks to the intensive efforts of conservationists and the productivity of Old Blue and her mate 'Old Yellow', there are now some 250 black robins alive today, and some have been returned to the now predator-free Pitt and Rangatira islands. One technique used in the recovery was to move the robin eggs firstly to the nests of tomtits, encouraging the robins to produce further broods. There was an initial problem with this in that the robins reared by tomtit foster parents developed identity crises – they sang tomtit songs and would not mate with other black robins. The conservationists devised a compromise where they moved the fledglings back to the robins' nest for 'finishing school'. Old Blue herself lived to be 13 years old, a tremendous age for a wild songbird. She is much celebrated in New Zealand as a true icon of conservation.

INTRODUCED SONGBIRDS

New Zealand has at least 17 species of introduced passerines. Many of them, such as the blackbird, song thrush, house sparrow and starling, are extremely common and seen throughout the country, especially in urban and agricultural areas to which they are well adapted. Slightly less common but widespread are such species as the skylark and dunnock. New Zealand is lacking in native seed-eating finches, so introduced goldfinches, greenfinches, chaffinches and redpolls have all prospered here. Rather less familiar to European or American eyes is the common myna. An import from Asia, it is a starling-sized bird with a brown body, dark grey-black head and yellow eye patch, and behaves very much like a starling. It is found only on North Island and is well adapted to urban life. In contrast the Australian magpie, a large black-and-white crow, prefers open farmland in both North and South islands where it is generally viewed as a pest.

Introduced passerines such as the goldfinch feed mainly on the seeds of introduced plant species. TDR

OTHER INTRODUCED LAND BIRDS

A number of large land birds have been brought to New Zealand as game or ornamental birds. Chief among the latter is the peacock (*Pavo cristatus*), which has gone feral in a number of locations in North Island, as has the wild turkey (*Meleagris gallopavo*). Game birds include the pheasant (*Phasianus colchicus*), grey partridge (*Perdix perdix*), red-legged partridge (*Alectoris rufa*), chukor (*Alectoris chukar*), brown bobwhite (*Coturnix ypsilophorus*) and California quail (*Callipepla californica*). This last is the commonest and also the smallest, with a rather ridiculous forward-curving crest like an attenuated quiff. Most of these have not been particularly successful apart from the pheasant and California quail. They do not appear to do any significant damage to the habitat, though they must have some impact, and do at least give hunters something other than native species to hunt.

MAMMALS

Bottle-nose dolphins TDR

For many years, scientists believed that no non-flying land mammals lived on New Zealand before the arrival of man, and that this gave rise to New Zealand's rightly celebrated diversity of birdlife.

However, in 2006 scientists announced the discovery of something that has challenged the status quo: some tiny fossil bones about 16 million years old. The pieces of jaw and thighbone, found in central Otago on South Island, appear to belong to a tiny, primitive mouse-sized mammal. How this species – which is neither marsupial nor 'conventional' mammal but an ancient predecessor of both – came to be on New Zealand is a mystery, but its discovery has supplied a fascinating new piece of the New Zealand wildlife jigsaw.

NATIVE LAND MAMMALS

Short-tailed bat. JK/DOC

Today there is no doubt about it. New Zealand's only native land mammals are two species of bats, which were able to fly across what is now the Tasman Sea from Australia after New Zealand separated from Gondwana. Both have since become different enough from their Australian ancestors to be distinct species. These two bats are not only few in numbers and nocturnal, but are also mainly forest-dwellers. The long-tailed bat (*Chalinolobus tuberculatus*) lives throughout the country and has fairly normal bat habits; if you see a bat flying above the canopy, it probably belongs to this species. The long-tailed bat may be a fairly recent arrival, being similar to several Australian species. The other species, the lesser short-tailed bat (*Mystacina tuberculata*) is more distinct from its Australian relatives. It is a fascinating animal, with several unusual habits. It is less frequently seen than the long-tailed bat as it lives almost entirely within the canopy. Though similar in size, it has larger ears and an unusual diet, feeding on nectar and berries, as well as insects. It has also developed the un-bat-like behaviour of foraging on the forest floor; its short tail and 'free' hind legs (not attached to the wings) give it the physical flexibility to accomplish this. This species is the specific pollinator of the parasitic root plant *Dactylanthus taylori*. It has a 'lek' breeding system, whereby the males gather together and sing for the females, who chose their mates based on their vocal ability. A third species, the greater short-tailed bat (*M. robusta*) is a recent casualty of introduced rats and stoats and is now extinct.

INTRODUCED LAND MAMMALS

New Zealand has, to its chagrin, over 30 species of introduced mammal. The first alien mammal to arrive was the kiore or Polynesian rat (*Rattus exulans*), which came over with the first Polynesian settlers some 750 years ago. Over the next 500 years it had a devastating impact on the native fauna, and is thought to have been directly responsible for the extinction of four species of flightless wren, a snipe and a snipe-rail, a number of frog species and several forest-floor beetles. Ironically the kiore itself is now quite rare in New Zealand, having been pushed out by the later introduction of its even more destructive cousins, the Norway or brown rat (*R. norvegicus*) and the ship or black rat (*R. rattus*).

While the arrival of the kiore spelt doom for many small ground-dwelling species, the Europeans made things considerably worse with a whole suite of destructive new mammals. Captain Cook brought pigs with him, and goats were put ashore at around the same time. It was common practice then for seamen to leave goats on islands to provide fresh meat for them on any future visit. More followed: most of the introductions were

Red deer do serious damage to native vegetation. NF

deliberate; the domestic mammals such as sheep, cows, horses, dogs and cats were part of the settlers' lives. But as the European settlements grew and more of the bush was cleared, more and more exotic animals were brought in.

There are now five species of wallaby (*Macropus* spp.) in New Zealand. These mostly have a fairly restricted range or are on islands. One, the white-throated wallaby (*M. parma*), is now rare in its native Australia and individuals have been captured on Kawau Island in the Hauraki Gulf and repatriated to Australia. The two that you might see are the red-necked wallaby (*M. rufogrisea*), which is found in the tussock grasslands of central South Island, and the dama or tammar wallaby (*M. eugenii*), which is found around Rotorua. Several of these, along with other alien animals and plants, were introduced by Sir George Grey, sometime governor and prime minister in the 19th century, who turned Kawau Island into something approaching a private zoo.

The animal importers were particularly keen on hoofed mammals (ungulates). Some of these, such as cows and horses, had clear practical purposes in farming and transport respectively, but many others, such as the seven species of deer, were purely for sport. Hunting is a national pastime, and red deer (*Cervus elaphus*) and Virginian or white-tailed deer (*Odocoileus virginiana*) are widespread. Higher up in the mountains you may see the two wild goats, the robust Himalayan tahr (*Hemitrageus jemlahicus*) and the handsome chamois (*Rupicapra rupicapra*), with its distinctive short, sharply back-curved horns. In all, people have brought in at least 12 species of ungulate, and all of these browsing and grazing animals are serious threats to the ecosystem. They target new growth and young plants and thus prevent regeneration of the native plant life, as well as spreading seeds of invasive grasses.

While the ungulates and wallabies are larger and more obvious, the brush-tailed possum (*Trichosorus vulpecular*) is more numerous, more widespread and much more damaging. It was introduced in 1858 in a bid to develop a fur industry for New Zealand. This never happened, but escapee possums have thoroughly exploited their new home. There are estimated to be over 70 million of them alive in New Zealand today, all munching their way through 35,000 tonnes of foliage per day – more than 12 million tonnes a year! The effect on many areas of forest has been catastrophic, with rata trees being a particular favourite. As they are nocturnal you

Stoats seriously threaten native birds, lizards and invertebrates.
AD/Tips

are most likely to see a possum in your car headlights or, even more likely, squashed on the road.

Other damaging introductions were the European rabbit (*Oryctolagus cuniculus*), introduced for meat, and the European or brown hare (*Lepus europaeus*) – less of a problem than the rabbit as it is fewer in numbers. The folly of introducing alien species to control already problematic aliens was amply illustrated by the introduction of stoats (*Mustela erminea*) and ferrets (*M. putorius*) to control rabbits. Both species do indeed hunt rabbits, but ground- and tree-nesting birds and native invertebrates are easier prey, as they have evolved without any need or means to protect themselves from such predators. You are most likely to see a stoat caught in a DOC trap while tramping though the bush.

The other introduced mammal that you may well see is the hedgehog (*Erinaceus europaeus*). Hedgehogs were introduced in an attempt to control garden pests, but like the stoats and ferrets they didn't read their job description properly and are more than happy to feast on native skinks, native invertebrates such as wetas and beetles, and the eggs of ground-nesting birds. They have become a serious threat to native wildlife in some areas.

New Zealand is an extremely good example of the damage that introduced species, especially mammals, can do to an ecosystem that developed without them. While progress is being made in the control and eradication of these pest species, this is largely focused on priority areas and offshore islands. There is no realistic chance of getting rid of those that are well established on the main islands, though a major rat and feral cat eradication programme has been initiated on Stewart Island.

TAKING ON THE ALIENS

As recently as the 1970s, scientists believed that the prospect of completely removing a population of introduced mammals from an island was remote at best. However, determined and inventive conservationists have found ways to make it happen. A multi-pronged attack, involving improved trapping technology, more effective poisons, anticoagulant baits, improved bait distribution and better overall planning, has enabled conservationists to successfully remove rodent populations from several of New Zealand's islands. House mice (*Mus musculus*) have now been eradicated from 13 islands of up to 7.1km², kiores from 32 islands up to 29.4km², black rats from 16 islands up to 1.6km², and Norway rats from 44 islands up to 113km². This largest island was Campbell Island, home to many breeding seabirds and also some unique land birds – sadly some of the latter had already been lost thanks to the rats. However, the Campbell Island teal was luckier. Extinct on its namesake island, this flightless duck still hung on in tiny numbers on nearby Dent Island. Captive breeding boosted its population, and in 2004 some of the birds were returned to a now rat-free Campbell Island, where they have since successfully bred.

Sperm whales always show their flukes when they dive. TDR

MARINE MAMMALS

In contrast to its lack of native land mammals, New Zealand has a healthy population of marine mammals, thanks to its extensive coastline. There are three main groups: whales, which are found mainly offshore; dolphins, which are more often inshore species; and seals and sea lions (pinnipeds), which breed or visit beaches around the coast. Over 40 species of cetacean (whales and dolphins) have been recorded in New Zealand waters.

WHALES

While many species of whale have been recorded, you are most likely to see one of three species. The largest of these is the sperm whale (*Physeter macrocephalus*), the world's largest toothed whale, which can be found year-round off Kaikoura on the east coast of South Island. Easily identifiable by its huge, towering square snout, like the front of a bus, as well as its forward-pointing blow and tiny vestigial dorsal fin, it comes to Kaikoura because of the squid and fish that are attracted by the upwellings of deep, nutrient-rich waters brought in by the 2,000–3,000m-deep undersea canyons just off the coast.

The other two species are both migratory. The southern right whale (*Eubalena australis*), so called because it was the 'right' whale to hunt, breeds in the Auckland and Campbell islands in the winter and is often seen off the coast of the main islands. The humpback whale (*Megaptera novaeangliae*) heads north up the east coast in the autumn to its tropical breeding grounds, and south down the west coast in spring to feed in the Antarctic. These two species are both filter-feeding baleen whales. They are of similar length, up to 16m long, but right whales are more heavily built, have no dorsal fin and often have clearly visible clusters of barnacles on their heads. Humpbacks have very knobbly protuberances on their head, extremely long flippers and are well known for making spectacular leaps or breaches, sometimes clear of the water.

The southern right whale is a regular visitor to coastal waters. TDR

DOLPHINS

There are six resident species of dolphin, and you should find it relatively easy to observe one or more of them as some stay in the same area year round. Largest is the orca (*Orcinus orca*), sometimes misleadingly referred to as 'killer whale'. Orcas are easy to identify with their distinctive black-and-white markings. They travel in pods of up to a dozen or so, with one dominant bull, who you'll recognise by his very tall dorsal fin, often a metre or more high, along with up to ten cows and juveniles. Orcas tend to have quite large territories and patrol around them. They can often be seen bottom-fishing for flatfish, or catching an eagle ray or other large fish. They will also happily take young sea lions or fur seals.

The other very large dolphin is the long-finned pilot whale (*Globicephala melas*), which is often wrecked on shore, especially on the very gently shelving beaches, often in large numbers. Techniques have been developed to help keep stranded whales and dolphins alive, and rescuers can now return many of them safely to their natural environment.

Orcas travel in family groups or pods. TDR

A dusky dolphin performing one of its habitual cartwheels. MJ

The endemic Hector's dolphin occurs mostly around South Island. TDR

Of the five smaller dolphins, the bottlenose (*Tursiops truncatus*) is a worldwide species, well known for playing around a boat's bow wave. Bottlenoses are found mainly at the northern ends of both main islands. The common dolphin (*Delphinus delphis*) is smaller, with distinctive white flank and belly markings; it occurs off Northland and down the east coast of North Island, often in very large schools. A dolphin with quite similar markings, but with a smoothly pointed rather than beaked face, is the dusky dolphin (*Lagenorhynchus obscurus*), well known for its dramatic acrobatic demonstrations. You may see dusky dolphins anywhere off the east coast from East Cape southwards, especially in Marlborough Sounds and off Kaikoura, where you can enjoy a swim with them.

New Zealand has one endemic dolphin. Hector's dolphin (*Cephalorhynchus hectori*) is the smallest of all dolphins at just 1.5m long, and has a diagnostic round dorsal fin. There are two subspecies: *C. h. hectori* which is found around South Island, and the critically endangered Maui dolphin *C. h. maui*, which has a population of only 150 individuals, all living around North island.

DOLPHIN DAYS

If you like swimming and have any affinity with the sea and its animals, you won't want to miss the opportunity to swim with dolphins when you visit New Zealand. There are a number of places where you can do this. Hauraki Gulf has regular visits from common and bottlenose dolphins and you have a 90% chance of successful viewing. Tauranga and Whakatane in the Bay of Plenty offer dolphin- and whale-watching and swimming trips. Kaikoura is the place for dusky dolphins, while Lyttleton and Akaroa offer the chance to swim with Hector's dolphin. From Manapouri and Te Anau you can book a marine wildlife cruise on Milford or Doubtful sounds, and swim with dolphins and seals. Any of these trips also offer the chance of close encounters with seabirds and other ocean wildlife.

The male New Zealand or Hooker's sea lion is much larger than the female. JF

SEALS AND SEA LIONS

This group of marine mammals is divided into the true seals or phocids, which have no visible external ears, and the eared seals or otarids, which do. While five phocids and three otarids may be found in New Zealand waters, only two species of otarid breed here. The commonest by far is the New Zealand fur seal (*Arctocephalus forsteri*), which breeds in small colonies all around the coast on rocky areas and beaches.

The New Zealand fur seal prefers rocky coasts. TDR

Southern elephant seals are easily identified by their enormous bulk. TDR

It has all-brown fur and a pointed, upturned nose. In contrast, the New Zealand or Hooker's sea lion (*Phocarctus hookeri*) is significantly larger, especially the males, which develop a thick ruff, and has much lighter fur. It prefers sandy beaches and sticks to the southeast of South Island as well as Stewart, Auckland and Campbell islands. This species is endangered in part because it frequently becomes entangled in fishermen's nets. In recognition of the hazard, there is a 'quota' that fishermen are permitted to catch without penalties, but this is a most unsatisfactory system, which neither the fishermen nor the conservationists are happy with.

If you are lucky you might come across a few other seals. Most likely is the huge elephant seal (*Mirounga leonine*), which (on land) looks more like a big grey sofa than an animal. Males can be up to 5m in length and weigh up to 3.5 tonnes. Less likely are the rather slim greyish leopard seal (*Hydrurga leptonyx*) and the sub-Antarctic fur seal (*Arctocephalus tropicalis*), which you can tell from the New Zealand fur seal by its pale face mask and Mohican crest.

94

Reptiles, Amphibians and Freshwater Fish

The Northland green gecko (*Naultinus greyii*) is endemic to New Zealand. HA/NV

Although New Zealand had some reptiles and amphibians on board when it began its life as a remote island group, they did not prove as successful as the birds and today's selection is small (though no less fascinating for that). New Zealand has a rather more diverse range of freshwater fish – unfortunately including a number of destructive non-natives.

REPTILES

New Zealand's reptiles are few in number, with several groups missing entirely. While there are some 80 species of gecko and skink, there are no snakes, no tortoises or freshwater turtles and no crocodiles, and the other major lizard groups are absent too. There are, however, some truly remarkable animals.

TUATARAS

If you want to see the most bizarre wildlife New Zealand has to offer, be sure to include these beguilingly wide-eyed reptiles on your list. The extraordinary tuataras (*Sphenodon* spp.) belong to an ancient family that was widespread during the age of reptiles. They are the only members of this family alive today, their nearest relatives having died out 60 million years ago, and they are often described as 'living fossils'. Though lizard-like in appearance, they actually represent a 'missing link' between snakes and lizards. Their unusual physiology includes a well-developed parietal or 'third' eye, and a tooth arrangement unlike that of any other living animal.

The tuatara is emblematic of New Zealand's amazing endemic wildlife. TDR

There are two species: *S. punctatus*, which lives only on a number of predator-free offshore islands; and Gunther's tuatara (*S. guntheri*), which is found only on the Brothers Islands in the Cook Straight. Tuataras were once widespread but loss of habitat and mammalian predators have reduced them to relict populations. You can, however, see them at Mount Bruce National Wildlife Centre and Karori Wildlife Sanctuary in Wellington.

GECKOS

You can tell geckos from New Zealand's other lizards, the skinks, by their rather rough-looking loose skin, often brightly coloured or patterned. There are at least 16 species from two groups: *Hoplodactylus* which are generally brown and nocturnal; and *Naultinus* which are generally green and diurnal (see page 95). New Zealand geckos do not lay eggs, but bear live young. There are four fairly common species that you may be fortunate enough to spot. The common gecko (*H. maculatus*), with dark and light brown patches, is

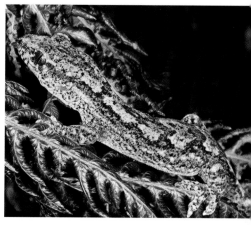

Geckos often hide under galvanised sheeting. TDR

widespread on both North and South islands and is found in forest, scrub and grassland to about 1,700m. The rather darker forest gecko (*H. granulatus*) has almost lichen-like colouration and is similarly widespread but is not found in grasslands. Two fairly common green geckos are the green tree gecko (*Nautilus elegans*) and the jewelled gecko (*N. gemmeus*). The former is green with irregular yellow markings and a blue gape (inside of the mouth), while the latter is smaller, with yellow lines running the length of its body, and a blue gape.

Thirty or more years ago, researchers in Fiordland discovered an alpine gecko, but not enough information was available to identify it. More recently further research has revealed that there are probably at least four species of alpine gecko, all with quite restricted ranges, and it seems likely that more species will be discovered as more surveys are made. So far these unusual geckos, which are found well above the tree line in areas with regular and severe frosts, have been found only on South Island and have not yet been fully described.

SKINKS

Skinks are shiny, smooth-skinned lizards that also differ from geckos in having clawed toes rather than padded ones, and in being entirely diurnal. Of more than 26 species of skink found in New Zealand, all are endemic apart from the smallest one, the rainbow skink (*Lampropholis delicata*), which was introduced from Australia and is found only in the northern half of North Island. Its tail is much longer, in

Skinks are easily identified by their shiny skin and clawed feet. TDR

relation to its body, than that of the native skinks. The common skink (*Oligosoma nigriplantare*) is widespread and quite easily identified: it is mid- to dark brown with two distinctive cream-coloured stripes running down its back. Another distinctive species, found only on North Island, is the copper skink (*Cyclodina aenea*). This is the smallest of the native skinks and can be found in coastal as well as inland areas, even in gardens. It is copper-coloured with paler flanks and irregular markings.

Not to be outdone by the geckos, skinks too are found in the alpine region. At least three species are known, of which one, the Otago skink (*Oligosoma otagense*), has a very dramatic black-and-cream colouration. The other two, the grand skink (*O. grande*) and the scree skink (*O. waimatense*), have very variegated markings: the former dark gold, the latter dark brown and cinnamon. Amazingly these skinks do not appear to hibernate, but have been observed in midwinter basking on wet rock surrounded by snow. We know little about their biology, but they are all endangered and a conservation programme is under way to protect them. If you see one and can photograph it you should report it to DOC.

AMPHIBIANS

New Zealand is home to just four native and three introduced amphibians, all frogs. The introduced species are not generally seen as pests as they do not compete directly with the natives; however, we have no clear idea of their impact on the ecosystem. All the native species, which are also endemic, are either vulnerable, endangered or critically endangered, and interestingly two of the aliens are also vulnerable or endangered in their native Australia.

The native frogs are very different from any frogs elsewhere. They are all less than 50mm long, lack external eardrums and do not croak but squeak. Their ribs are not attached to their backbones and they cannot extend their tongues to catch prey. They are nocturnal and thus hard to observe, and extremely restricted in their range – mainly to predator-free island nature reserves. The native species you are most likely to see is Hochstetter's frog (*Leiopelma hochstetteri*), which is found in a number of scattered sites in native bush from East Cape to Waikato and southern

Northland. The other three native species are very hard to observe: the critically endangered Archey's frog (*L. archeyi*) is found only in upland scrub in Coromandel and Waikato; Hamilton's frog (*L. hamiltoni*) is restricted to Stephen's Island in Cook Straight, with a few recently translocated to the Chetwode Islands; and the Maud Island frog (*L. pakeka*) is found only on Maud Island and a few other predator-free islands in the Marlborough Sounds. All three are non-aquatic, do not have webbed feet and carry their young around on their backs.

The frogs you are much more likely to see, and hear, are the three introduced Australian species. The smallest is the whistling or brown tree frog (*Litoria ewingii*), which is larger than the native species and is found mainly on South Island and the west of North Island; its call is a rather cricket-like 'weeep weeep weeep'. The two others are much larger. The attractive bright green and gold bell frog (*L. aurea*) can be up to 90mm long, and has webbed hind feet and climbing pads on all toes and fingers. It is found only in the northern half of North Island. The southern bell frog (*L. raniformis*) is larger, up to 100mm, and is a much darker green with brown rather than gold markings; it has no suckers on fingers or toes. This is the most widespread frog but is unlikely to be found in areas of native bush.

It is thought that there were at least seven native species of frog within historic times, and while significant conservation effort is going into the preservation of the remaining native species, the two biggest dangers are, as usual, the loss of habitat and the introduced predators. The threat is greatest to Archey's frog, which has been classified as an EDGE species, one that is Evolutionarily Distinct and Globally Endangered.

The Maud Island frog is nocturnal and does not have webbed feet. TDR

FRESHWATER AND ESTUARINE FISH

New Zealand has 41 native species of fish, most of them endemic. There are also over 20 non-native species, including seven species of salmon and trout, as well as carp, perch, tench, goldfish and guppy, all of which were deliberately introduced, largely for sport. We do not know how much introduced species affect the ecology of the rivers, but as they prey on native species, they are unlikely to be beneficial. Conservationists suspect them of contributing to the only known extinction of a native fish species, the upokororo or grayling (*Prototroctes oxyrhynchus*), which was last recorded in the 1920s. Three families of fish dominate New Zealand's rivers.

Giant kokopu AM/NSI

GALAXIIDS

Of the 41 species of natives, 22 are from the family Galaxiidae, the name deriving from their sparkly silver or gold spotting which resembles stars in a galaxy. Five species of this family – the giant, shortjaw and banded kokopus, the inanga and the koaro (*Galaxias argenteus, G. postvectis, G. fasciatus, G. maculatus* and *G. brevipinnis*) – are migratory and their immatures are collectively referred to as whitebait. Their annual upstream migration in the spring disrupts normal life throughout the country. Catching them (whitebaiting) is a national pastime and, as with other outdoor pursuits in New Zealand, the practitioners take it quite seriously. The life cycle of these fish is intriguing. The adults migrate downstream to spawn in the estuaries in the autumn. The spawning is timed for the autumnal spring tides, generally the highest of the year, with the eggs being deposited in the grasses that ring the shoreline. The eggs hatch at the next or the spring tides after that, and the larval fish head out to sea for the winter. In the spring they return to the estuaries and head upriver, dodging, hopefully, the numerous nets set for them by the fishers.

A galaxiid can be identified most easily by its single dorsal fin, set far back on the body, almost directly above the anal fin. These fish have two sets of pectoral fins, which enable them to accelerate quickly. They are not great long-distance swimmers, though some species are good at 'climbing' the rocks as they head upstream. Whitebait, being immature, are small, measuring no more than 50mm, but the adults are appreciably larger. Mature adults of the giant kokopu can grow to over 400mm and weigh over 1kg with a lifespan of over 20 years.

EELS

Another notable migratory freshwater fish family is that of the eels. Three species of the family Anguillidae are found in New Zealand: one of them, the longfin eel (*Anguilla diefenbachii*), is endemic; a second, the shortfin eel (*A. australis*), is native and widespread throughout the South Pacific. The third, the Australian longfin or spotted eel (*A. reinhardtii*), is a fairly recent arrival, probably since 1980, and is restricted to a few North Island rivers.

The longfin eel is probably the largest eel in the world and may live for 30 years. TE

Shortfin eels are distinguished by their shorter dorsal fin, which is of a similar length to the anal fin, while the longfin eel has a dorsal fin extending well forward to the anal fin. The Australian longfin can be distinguished from its endemic counterpart by irregular dark markings on the back and sides. Shortfin eels tend to remain fairly close to the coast, but longfins are well known for their 'climbing' ability and can be found far inland. Both native species are widespread on all three main islands, though the impact of angling and commercial fisheries has reduced stocks, especially of very large specimens. The longfin is probably the largest eel in the world and is known to grow to nearly 2m in length and weigh up to 24kg. Eels are generally nocturnal and are the top predators in the rivers and lakes – there is even a report of one taking an Australasian shoveler duck. Shortfin eels rarely exceed 1m in length.

The eel's life cycle is similar to, but more complex than, that of the whitebait galaxiids. Mature adults descend the rivers but swim off to tropical waters to the north of New Zealand, where they spawn and die. The transparent leaf-shaped larvae drift on the ocean currents, which finally bring them back to New Zealand. Once in coastal water they develop the familiar eel shape but remain colourless – at this stage they are known as glass eels. As they grow they develop a brown pigment and are known as elvers, at which point they ascend the rivers and spend the next 20 or 30 years maturing before descending to spawn and die. Females may live for more than 30 years, while males are less long-lived. Reports of 100-year-old eels are unsubstantiated.

INTRODUCED FISH AND FISHING

Once European settlers became established in New Zealand, they brought in freshwater fish for sport, as the native fish were not very sporting. There are now more than 20 introduced species of freshwater fish established in New Zealand. Two species of Asian carp, the grass carp (*Cyprinuis carpio*) and the silver carp (*Hypophthalmichthys molitris*), are unable to breed here but are used to control lake weed and algal blooms in lakes and drainage ditches. Agricultural run-off of nitrogen and phosphates is the direct cause of algal blooms and also contributes to the growth of introduced aquatic weeds.

The most widespread introduced sports fish are the brown trout (*Salmo trutta*) and the rainbow trout (*Orcorhynchus mykiss*). In South Island rivers you can find chinook salmon (*O. tshawytscha*) and there are a few landlocked Atlantic salmon (*Salmo salar*) in South Island lakes. While you can catch both salmon and trout for sport, you are not allowed to sell or raise trout commercially. There are a number of salmon farms where you can fish your own salmon. Freshwater fishing is regulated by Fish and Game New Zealand who issue licences. For the avid fly fisher, New Zealand offers a lot of opportunities.

Male bluegill bully in breeding display. AM/NSI

BULLIES

The other common freshwater fish family is the Eleotridae or bullies, not to be confused with the saltwater cockabullies. There are seven species of bully in New Zealand, all of the genus *Gobiomorphus*, and all endemic. They are small, dark-coloured fish with two rounded dorsal fins. Three species live entirely in freshwater, including upland and sub-alpine rivers and lakes, while the others have a migratory reproductive cycle, with the young spending some time in salt water. The two largest are the common bully (*G. cotidiana*) and the giant bully (*G. gobioides*), both of which can grow to 150mm long and are virtually indistinguishable in the field. Both are migratory, though the giant bully rarely ventures far inland. The other two migratory species are the smallest of the family, the bluegill bully (*G. hubbsi*) and the redfin bully (*G. huttoni*), both of which can be identified by their colouration.

OTHER FRESHWATER FISH

A fish that you could mistake for an eel is the parasitic lamprey (*Geotria australis*) about whose life cycle we have surprisingly little knowledge. The adults attach themselves to other fish by their sucker-like mouths, and feed on the host's flesh. Lampreys migrate in the opposite direction to most other native species, the adults travelling upriver to spawn. The young then spend several years in the rivers, probably feeding on small invertebrates before returning to the sea where they latch onto a suitable host fish. There are also two endemic species of smelt, and one member of the Pinguipedidae or cod family. This is the torrentfish (*Cheimarricthys fosteri*), a small brown fish which is adept at living in fast-flowing streams, but surprisingly is not very good at climbing and does not penetrate to the upper reaches of rivers. It too spends part of its life cycle in estuaries, but its actual breeding behaviour is unknown.

ESTUARINE FISH

There are five native species that are more correctly described as estuarine, as they live most of their lives in the tidal waters of estuaries, although they also spend some of their life cycle further up the rivers. These include two mullets, the globally common grey mullet (*Mugil cephalus*) and the yellow-eyed mullet (*Aldrichetta forsteri*); one flatfish, the black flounder (*Rhombosolea retiaria*); and one triplefin, the estuarine triplefin (*Grahamina nigripenne*), so named because of its three dorsal fins. The last of these belongs to quite a large family, the rest of which are marine.

INVERTEBRATES

Nursery-web spider NF

Although New Zealand is not widely noted for its invertebrate fauna, and while invertebrates may not be top of every visitor's 'must see' list, the country does offer opportunities to observe and appreciate a wide range of forms and species, many of them unknown elsewhere. Invertebrates comprise 95% of known animal species on the planet and are an integral and vital part of the ecosystem. There are thought to be some 80,000 invertebrate species here, including over 10,000 beetles. As with other areas of the natural history, there is a large degree of endemism. Most species will be new and full of wonder to the discerning visitor, and very few will bite or sting – in sharp contrast to Australia which is replete with dangerous creepy-crawlies. In fact, the most dangerous living things in New Zealand are plants: the bush lawyer (*Rubus cissoids*) with is myriad back-curving hooks, and the tree nettle (*Urtica ferox*), with its impressive array of sharp, stinging spines. There are no poisonous snakes, in fact no snakes at all, and no scorpions. The only animals that might cause pain are the sandflies of the west coast, four species of spider (three of them imported from Australia), a centipede, and a few imported bees and wasps.

As the top native New Zealand predators were birds, reptiles or insects, which tend to use sight and movement to locate their prey, many native invertebrates are nocturnal and freeze when in danger. Neither strategy is any defence against mammals, which use smell as well as sight to locate their prey. It is estimated that up to 20% of native invertebrates (some 16,000 species) are threatened; some may already be extinct.

In addition to the natives, there are in excess of 2,000 introduced invertebrates, with more arriving all the time in spite of biosecurity precautions. How do you effectively inspect the 500,000 shipping containers that arrive every year for tiny passengers? These aliens are sometimes innocuous, but many will become established and impact on native species and the ecosystem. Several, such as the European wasps and Argentine ants, have become pests and seriously threaten native species.

Powelliphanta snails are very large and carnivorous.
TDR

Make sure you do not add to the invasion by taking great care not to bring alien species with you or transport any invertebrates around the country.

SNAILS AND VELVET WORMS

They may not be everyone's favourite tourist attraction, but in New Zealand there are a number of particularly interesting snails, most notably the giant land snails. The largest of them, *Powelliphanta superba*, can have a shell up to 100mm in diameter. Somewhat smaller are the kauri snails (*Paryphanta* spp.), which can be up to 75mm in diameter. Giant land snails and kauri snails are both carnivorous and feed mainly on earthworms and other soil invertebrates. Both are found in native forest, the kauri snails in the north of North Island and *Powelliphanta* in southern North Island and throughout South Island. Other large snails found in the north are the vegetarian flax snails (*Placostylus* spp.). These have spiral shells which can be up to 80mm high. All are at serious risk from habitat loss and mammalian predators.

Peripatus or velvet worms are truly peculiar animals which look like large flattened caterpillars. Some species of the genus *Peripatoites* can grow to 80mm in length. They have a soft, velvety, un-segmented body, 14–16 pairs of stumpy legs and two large antennae. They vary in colour from rather dull earthy tones to indigo blue and black with yellow spots. They are carnivorous, feeding on other invertebrates and catching their prey by ensnaring it with a sticky gum-like substance that they eject from openings beside the mouth. Their name stems from the Greek 'periplus', which translates as 'a sailing around' or 'an ongoing journey', from their apparently restless nature.

SPIDERS

There are estimated to be around 3,000 species of spider in the country, but only around a third of them have been fully described. The large majority are endemic but, as is so often the case here, it is often the introduced species that you see most frequently as they are adapted to the pastoral and urban landscape that covers so much of the country.

Among the commoner spiders are the nursery-web spider (*Dolomedes minor*), a large, pale brown creature. It carries its egg sac around with it until the eggs hatch, whereupon the parent constructs a dense web at the ends of a branch, typically gorse or manuka, where the young develop and grow. Another spider you're likely to see is the common orb web spider (*Eriophora pustulosa*) which has a distinctive spiky abdomen and constructs an orb-shaped web to catch its prey. Much smaller but easily identified is the black-headed jumping spider (*Trite planiceps*) – its large eyes help it spot and attack its prey by jumping on it. The largest spider found is the Avondale huntsman (*Delena cancerides*), a pale grey-brown Australian import found mainly in Auckland and Waikato.

The black-headed-jumping spider can jump up to 50cm. NF

More widespread than the Avondale is the native black tunnelweb spider (*Porrhothele antipodiana*), a large reddish, very heavy-bodied spider, often found under rocks, in log piles and in gardens or even indoors. It builds a web tunnel from which it appears to attack passing prey. Courting males entering the females' web tunnel run the risk of being devoured by their intended mates.

Black tunnelweb spider NF

While almost all spiders are potentially poisonous, some have such small fangs that they are unable to pierce human skin, others have relatively innocuous venom, and only two, the katipos, are classified as poisonous – though their bite is not lethal. These small black spiders are restricted to sandy beaches in the north of the country, especially around the bases of spinifex and marram grasses. Two other spiders classed as poisonous are two Australian imports, the red-backed spider (*Lampona hasselti*), which is similar but slightly larger than the katipos, and the white-tailed spider (*L. cylindrata*), which has a steely grey abdomen with a white patch at the end.

Other spiders to keep an eye open for are the sheetweb spiders (*Cambridgeana* spp.), whose low, spreading webs you will probably notice when tramping through the bush; the slater spider (*Dysdera crocota*), with pale grey abdomen and reddish thorax and legs, so named as it preys almost exclusively on woodlice or slaters; and the daddy longlegs spider (*Pholcus phalagioides*), which has a very small pale grey body and extremely long legs, especially the front pair, which it uses to entrap its prey in silk. Daddy longlegs spiders are very common in houses, especially in North Island.

CENTIPEDES AND MILLIPEDES

Centipedes and millipedes have many-segmented bodies. Centipedes are somewhat flattened and have one pair of legs on each segment; millipedes are generally rounded and have two pairs of legs for each body segment. There are around 40 species of centipede in New Zealand, mostly of them less than 50mm long. They are found mainly in the earth, detritus and under rocks and logs. The largest native centipede is *Cormocephalus rubriceps*, which grows to 20cm in length. Centipedes are carnivores and have specially adapted legs called forcipules with which they catch and paralyse their prey, While they can give you a painful nip they are shy, retiring animals and unless you pick them up they are unlikely to bite you.

There are probably several hundred species of millipede, only 60 of them described, and also 12 introduced species which are common in gardens. Millipedes have few defences apart from their hard exoskeletons and, in some species, the ability to curl into a ball. As with centipedes, you have to search for them in soil detritus and rotting logs. They feed on plant matter, especially leaves and wood, and are important agents in the breaking down of this material, especially the wood, in the soil.

INSECTS

Insects are often the most obvious of the invertebrates that we encounter. Almost everyone notices flies, bees, wasps, butterflies and moths – but the range of insects on display in New Zealand is a great deal more varied than that and includes some 6–10,000 species of beetle. At least 90% of New Zealand's insects are endemic.

LAND BEETLES

Beetles are mostly shy and retiring by nature, which means that you will often have to look for them. Under rocks and logs are good places to start. Native beetles are largely nocturnal and adapted to forest life, but they can be found anywhere from the coast to altitudes of 3,700m and even next to hot springs. So keep your eyes open and do a bit of fossicking. There are six major families represented.

Longhorn beetles (Cerambycidae)

Longhorn beetles are so named for their very long antennae, which are sometimes much longer than the body. This is the case with the largest of them – the huhu beetle (*Prionoplus reticularis*), which is up to 40mm long and squeaks. Two other longhorns, the spiny longhorn (*Blosyropus spinosus*), which is longer but much slimmer, and the kanuka longhorn (*Ochrocydus huttoni*), which is pale brown, are quite common, as is the introduced burnt-pine longhorn (*Arhopalus tristis*), which is about 30mm long with an abdomen that protrudes beyond its wing cases. The grubs of longhorn beetles eat dead or rotten wood. The larger ones may find themselves on the human menu, raw or fried; they are also sometimes used as fish bait.

Scarab, chafer and dung beetles (Scarabaeidae)

Scarabs have a characteristic dumpy, oval shape and often very shiny wing cases. The largest of them is the large sand scarab or mumutawa (*Pericoptus truncatus*), a coastal beetle with shiny, rich-brown wing cases that burrows in the sand during the day and is found from Christchurch northwards. Very similar but smaller are the small sand scarabs (*Pericoptusa* spp.), which are more numerous in some areas. Black scarab beetles are likely to be introduced Mexican dung beetles (*Copris incertis*), the male of which has a small horn; or the rather smaller black beetle (*Heteronychus arator*). Two handsome green chafer beetles are the mumu chafer (*Stethapsis longicornis*), found in the northern half of North Island, and the tanguru chafer (*S. suturalis*), which is widespread and has a yellow stripe on the edges of its wing cases where they meet. Much smaller is the manuka chafer or kekerewai (*Pyronita festiva*), which has both a green and an orange form. Scarab grubs feed on plant roots.

The bright green mumu chafer is one of New Zealand's more distinctive beetles. JF

Ladybirds (Coccinellidae)

Most people are familiar with these very small, often brightly coloured beetles. Three native species that you may find are the red-and-black flax ladybird (*Cassiculus venustus*), found on flax plants in North Island; the handsome orange-spotted ladybird (*Cocinella leonina*) which is widespread and sports 16 orange spots on a black background; and the rather dull brown Antipodean ladybird (*Harmonia antipodia*) which is restricted to North Island. Other ladybirds that you see are likely to be introduced species such as the two-spotted ladybird (*Adalia bipunctata*), or the 11-spotted ladybird (*Cocinella undecimpunctata*). Introduced ladybirds can be beneficial as they prey on aphids, mealy bugs and scale insects, most of which were also imported.

Weevils (Curculionidae)

The weevils make up another large family and are best identified by their rather long snouts. They often have antennae that grow out at right angles, and then bend forward again. Of more than 1,500 species found here, the most remarkable and the largest is the giraffe weevil or tuwhaipapa (*Lasiorhynchus barbicornis*), the male of which is 70mm long, the longest beetle in New Zealand. Almost half of this prodigious length is an extremely long 'snout', with a pair of long antennae sticking out at right angles close to its tip. The female is much smaller and has the antenna nearer the base of the snout, which enables her to bore into wood to lay her eggs. Most other weevils, native and introduced, are much smaller, no more than 20mm long. Some have very specialised lifestyles, such as the introduced gorse seed weevil (*Exapion ulicis*). This creature feeds only on the seed pods of gorse, and was introduced to help control this invasive introduced plant. The endemic flightless flax weevil (*Anagotus fairburni*) and the five-finger weevil (*Ectopsis ferrugalis*) are also specialist feeders that live on just one specific species of plant.

Ground beetles (Carabidae)

This group includes some of the commonest beetles. There are over 400 species in New Zealand and most are flightless and endemic. They are mostly black or dark brown and often have clearly visible jaws. Their body is longer and more slender than the rotund scarabs. One common native species is the stinking ground beetle (*Plocamostethus planiusculus*). Don't be tempted to pick it up: it can leave a terrible smell, and give you a painful nip into the bargain. The metallic ground beetle (*Megadromus antarcticus*) is widespread, especially in South Island, and frequently turns up in gardens.

Stag beetles (Lucanidae)

These are rather less well represented, with only 30 species. They are all-black, quite bulky and often flightless; most of the natives are endemic. The largest stag beetle is Helm's stag beetle (*Geodorcus helmsi*). The male is up to 30mm long with a massive pair of jaws; this species prefers the wetter western regions, especially Fiordland. Earl's stag beetle (*Dendroblax earlii*) is another endemic species but is flighted and

This black ground beetle is one of 150 similar native species. JF

looks rather more like a scarab or chafer beetle, but with clearly visible jaws. A number of introduced species have also made it here, particularly from Australia.

FLIES

Flies are generally regarded as more of a nuisance than something to look out for, unless you happen to be an entomologist. New Zealand has over 600 native species, including several crane flies, the largest of which is the giant crane fly (*Austropitula hudsoni*), followed by the equally long-legged but smaller-bodied mountain crane fly (*Leptotarsus montanus*). There are several mosquitoes, one of which, the saltpool mosquito (*Opifex fuscus*), breeds in seawater. Also less than welcome are the sandflies or namus (*Austrosimulium* spp.), which can be extremely unpleasant. Watch out for these – especially in Westland and Fiordland in the summer. Rather less of a problem but much noisier are blowflies, especially the endemic New Zealand blue blowfly (*Calliphora quadrimaculata*). Probably the most interesting fly is the endemic titiwai or puratoke (*Arachynocampa luminosa*), whose scientific name reveals that it is the adult form of the New Zealand glow-worm. There are a number of caves, shaded cliffs and riverbanks where you can view these, most notably at Waitomo. The larvae live in a tube-like nest and send out a large number of sticky 'fishing lines' to entrap their prey, which are attracted by bioluminescence emitted from each larva's tail. Seeing a cliff or bank studded with these tiny lights, you can easily imagine you're looking at a distant city, so numerous and far away do they seem.

BEES AND WASPS

Bees are essentially hairy vegetarian wasps. Both are members of the order Hymenoptera, 'insects with narrow waists', and both are divided into two groups, those that live in colonies ('social') and those that live on their own ('solitary'). There are no native social bees or wasps, but there are 28 solitary bee species, three of which do show some social tendencies. There are some 2,000–3,000 wasp species, many of them very small. There are also, as usual, numerous introduced species, most notably the social honeybee (*Apis mellifera*), and various solitary bumblebees

The introduced Chinese paper wasp feeds on native invertebrates. JF

(*Bombus* spp.). All the introduced bees are important pollinators, especially of introduced plants, as native bees do not have long enough tongues to do the job. There are four introduced social wasp species. Two are Europeans: the German wasp (*Vespula germanica*) and the common wasp (*V. vulgaris*), both of which are pest species and cause problems with their love of 'honeydew' (see box opposite). The other two introduced species are paper wasps: the Chinese paper wasp (*Polistes chinensis*) and the Australian paper wasp (*P. humilis humilis*), both of which are much slimmer than the European wasps and are more obviously narrow-waisted.

Native bees are not dissimilar in appearance to the honey-bee, but all are a lot smaller and generally darker coloured. Many of them are from the genus *Leiproctus* and are very hard to tell apart. They nest in tunnels in mudbanks, often close together, giving the impression of a small colony.

The native wasps fall into several families. Most commonly seen are the solitary hunting wasps which have generally dark abdomens, often clear or reddish-brown wings, and a lifestyle that some people may find disturbing. The large black hunting wasp (*Priocnemis monachus*) is widespread and hunts primarily tunnelweb and trapdoor spiders. When she finds a spider the female paralyses it with a sting, drags it to an excavated tunnel, lays an egg on it and seals up the hole. The egg hatches, the grub eats the paralysed spider then pupates and finally emerges as a new adult. The mason wasp (*Pison spinolae*) is smaller but also widespread and preys mainly on orbweb spiders. Rather than dig a hole, the female builds a nest out of mud, often in keyholes or elsewhere indoors, to which she carries the spider as food for the larva.

The parasitic ichneumon wasps are much larger. The females are clearly identifiable by their long ovipositors, which are used to lay eggs in their prey – often a beetle grub deep within rotting wood. The largest of them is the native giant ichneumon wasp (*Certonotus fractinervis*), with a body up to 35mm long and an ovipositor up to 50mm long. Rather smaller and darker is the endemic lemon tree borer (*Xanthocryptus novozealandicus*). Closely related to the wasps are the sawflies and wood wasps. There are some ten species of these quite large flying insects – they also have clearly visible ovipositors, but are much more heavily built than the ichneumon wasps.

SAP-SUCKERS AND HONEYDEW

In many beech woods, especially on South Island, and especially on the black beech (*Nothofagus solandri*), you will notice that the trunk appears to be covered with a black mould. This is just what it is – and it is there because underneath are numerous sap-sucking aphids (*Ultracoelostoma* spp.), which produce a sweet liquid known as honeydew. The insects excrete 'alimentary waste fluid' through a long slender white anal tube, which extends 5mm or more from the trunk. The liquid drips out of the tube onto the trunk, hence the mould, which helpfully covers up the aphid, protecting it from potential predators. In high summer, trees can be covered with these white, hair-like tubes as the aphids churn out vast quantities of honeydew – an important food for many forest bird species.

European wasps feeding on honeydew from the sooty beech scale insect. JF

Honeydew is an important food source for many native insects too. It has also been targeted by beekeepers who produce a very tasty 'honeydew honey' from their bees that feed on the honeydew. Unfortunately the introduced German and common wasps have also discovered this cornucopia of free food and feed on it in their thousands, preventing native species and even honeybees from feeding. This is potentially a serious problem as many native birds are nectar-feeders and the loss of this source of food will inevitably affect population numbers. Additionally the increased numbers of alien wasps may well impact seriously on native invertebrates, on which the wasps also feed.

ANTS

Ants of the family Formacidae belong to the same group as the bees and wasps (Hymenoptera). This is one of the most successful insect families, with some 20,000 species worldwide. There are 40 species in New Zealand, of which only eight are native and all of those endemic, including one endemic genus (*Huberia*). The native ants are generally found in areas of native forest and are hard to tell apart without a microscope. In urban and agricultural areas you are more likely to encounter introduced ants. Largest is probably the southern Michelin ant (*Ambylopone australis*) which is 8–9mm long and anything from dark yellow to black in colour. It nests in small colonies under logs and stones. More common, especially on my desk, is the 2mm-long black house ant (*Ochetellus glaber*), which is widespread in gardens and houses, as is the white-footed house ant (*Technomyrmex albipies*). More serious pest ants are the Argentine ant (*Linepithium humile*), which may form very large colonies that can be unpleasant to humans, but, more importantly, extremely damaging to the native wildlife, especially invertebrates. Even more dangerous is the tiny and very aggressive little red fire ant (*Solenopsis invicta*) which packs an amazing punch for its size and is extremely damaging environmentally, attacking birds and reptiles in addition to invertebrates. While it has been reported in New Zealand it is thought not to have become established. Please report any suspected sightings or bitings to DOC.

WETAS

Wetas are among the animal wonders of New Zealand. They are members of the order Orthoptera, which includes grasshoppers and crickets, all of which have large hind legs adapted for jumping. There are over 100 species of weta, all endemic and split into two families. The Rahaphidophoridae or cave wetas have small bodies but very long legs, and the Anostostomatidae (giant, tusked, tree and ground wetas) have heavy bodies and shorter legs. The largest of them are the giant wetas (*Deinacridia* spp.), of which there are 11 species with distinct geographical distributions. The heaviest recorded is the wetapunga (*D. heteracantha*) from Little Barrier Island in the Hauraki Gulf; it can be up to 75mm long and weigh over 70g,

three times the weight of a mouse; its hind legs are up to 130mm long. Wetapunga translates as 'god of ugly things' and wetas are, to many of us, ugly and sometimes ferocious-looking. The males of the giant tusked wetas (*Motuweta* spp.) and of the tree wetas (*Hemideina* spp.) have large, fearsome jaws. Both tusked and tree wetas are omnivorous. When alarmed the tusked weta can jump a considerable distance but the tree weta raises its very spiny hind legs vertically in a surprisingly effective threat display, I was quite startled the first time I witnessed it! The amazing alpine weta (*H. maori*) lives in the mountains of South Island and is known to freeze solid and recover when the temperature rises, with no ill effects. Smallest in the family are the ground wetas (*Hemiandrus* spp.) which are only 25–30mm long and live in holes in the ground. Females of all species can be distinguished from males by their long curved ovipositors. All species have remarkable long antennae, often more than twice the length of the animal.

Despite its fearsome appearance, this tree weta is harmless. TDR

The cave wetas or tokoriro, of which there are some 50 species, have much

Cave wetas are generally seen in groups and have amazingly long antennae. TDR

smaller, slimmer bodies, generally up to 30mm long, but their hind legs may be up to 90mm long and their forelegs 45mm. They also have immensely long antennae, up to four times their body length. They are good jumpers and are largely vegetarian but do eat some invertebrates. They can be found in caves, unused buildings and under vegetation or boulders, from the coast to over 3,000m.

All New Zealand wetas are nocturnal and flightless and, as we have seen elsewhere, this was an effective survival strategy before the arrival of mammals. Their populations have since been severely depleted by rodents and mustelids, with the result that some species survive only on predator-free offshore islands.

WETA HOTELS
One of the problems in observing wetas in the wild is that they are nocturnal and adept at hiding themselves away during the day. To get round this problem, a number of reserves and sanctuaries – including Karori and Tiritiri Matangi – have built 'weta hotels'. These are small tree trunks that are split in half, with one side hollowed out to provide passageways and larger areas for wetas to hide in. This side is then covered with a clear perspex sheet, while the other half is hinged onto it and held closed with a clasp. Around dawn the wetas find the entrance hole, climb up and go to sleep in the bark chambers. You can then come along, undo the clasp, open the log, and there are the wetas safe behind their perspex window – a wonderfully simple and very educational idea.

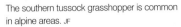

The southern tussock grasshopper is common in alpine areas. JF

Black field crickets appear in late summer and can be very noisy. JF

GRASSHOPPERS AND CRICKETS

In comparison with the remarkable wetas, the related grasshoppers and crickets are a little unimpressive. There are around 20 species of grasshopper and ten crickets, mostly endemic. Grasshoppers are found mainly in native grassland. The New Zealand grasshopper (*Phaulacridium marginale*) is found mainly in lowland grasslands, while the two tussock grasshoppers, the northern (*Paprides nitidus*) and the southern (*Sigaus australis*), are generally found above 1,000m. All are quite small, up to 30mm long. Slightly larger is the North Island grasshopper (*S. pilliferus*), which is endangered. Largest of all at 50–60mm is the migratory locust (*Locusta migratoria*), a worldwide species found in sand dunes and rough grasslands south as far as Christchurch. It does not swarm in New Zealand – this behaviour is reserved for warmer climates.

You are more likely to hear a cricket than to see one, but the commonest by far is the native black field cricket or pihareinga (*Teleogryllus comodus*), which is almost black and 20–30mm long, the female with a long curved ovipositor. It is found south as far as Kaikoura and is most likely to be heard singing in the late summer and autumn. It is flighted and occasionally swarms.

BUTTERFLIES

In spite of being winged, surprisingly few butterflies have made it across the Tasman. This paucity could be to do with the fact that butterflies are normally diurnal and less well adapted to a land of birds. Recent research has indicated that there may be some 60 species of native butterfly, almost all endemic, plus a number of species that get blown here from time to time. There are also four introduced species, including our old friend the small or cabbage white (*Pieris rapae*). The largest butterfly you are likely to see is the monarch or kahukyu (*Danaus plexippus*), a worldwide species that is thought to have arrived here of its own accord in about 1870. It is unmistakable with its black and burnt-ochre colouring; the males can be identified by two small dark marks on their hind wings (these are scent glands). The caterpillar is dramatically coloured with white, yellow and black bands. Two fairly widespread endemic species are the red admiral or kahukura (*Vanessa gonerilla gonerilla*), and the yellow admiral or kahukowhai (*V. itea*). A regular non-breeding visitor is the Australian painted lady (*V. kershawi*). There are six species of endemic ringlet; most easily seen are the three species of tussock ringlet (*Argyophenga* spp.). All are two-tone brown with distinctive wing spots. Less common and difficult to spot is the darker forest ringlet (*Dodonidia helmii*), and there are also two mountain species, of which the black mountain ringlet (*Percnodaimon merula*) is the most likely to be seen.

The red admiral is common in gardens. JF

The largest group of butterflies is the family Lycaenidae – the blues and coppers. Just to confuse you, the male of the boulder copper (*Boldenaria boldenarum*) is not copper-coloured but blue, with black marks in the middle of each wing. Two of the three native blues, the long-tailed blue (*Lampides boeticus*) and the common blue (*Zizinia labradus*) are fairly recent arrivals, while the endemic southern blue (*Z. otis oxleyi*) is significantly smaller. The common copper or pepeparariki (*Lycaena salustius*) is the largest of the family, although it is variable and may actually consist of several species. The same applies to the glade copper (*L. feredayi*), which is found along forest margins.

The common copper is often seen feeding on introduced thistles. JF

The native magpie moth has smaller white spots than its Australian counterpart. NF

MOTHS

While there are relatively few species of butterfly in New Zealand, there are more than 1,700 of moth, ranging from the very large puriri moth or pepetuna (*Aenetus virescens*) which has bright green forewings and a wingspan of up to 150mm, down to the tiny pond moth (*Hygraula nitens*) at only 15mm. Moths can be distinguished from butterflies by three main features. Butterflies hold their wings together above their backs or spread flat out, while moths generally lay them flat along their body with the front wings covering the back wings. Butterflies are generally diurnal while moths are generally nocturnal but, diagnostically, butterflies have club-tipped antennae while virtually all moths do not.

Moths are often masters of camouflage and one that is an expert is the cabbage tree moth (*Epiphryne verriculata*). It has a wingspan of some 60mm and is patterned with horizontal reddish-brown and pale brown lines that help it to blend in to the veins on the dead leaves of the cabbage tree. There are also a number of lichen moths (*Declana* spp.) that have dramatic patterns to camouflage them when they are resting on lichen.

Many moths have eye-like markings on their wingtips, including the 170 species of owlet moths. The largest of these belong to the genus *Dasypodia*,

The introduced cinnabar moth has bold black and crimson markings NF

have wingspans of up to 80mm and are introduced from Australia. The native silver Y (*Chysodeixis erisoma*) is widespread and easy to identify by the silver 'Y'-shaped marking on the forewing. Hawkmoths are surprisingly poorly represented, with just one native species, the convolvulus hawk or hihue (*Agrius convolvuli*), a dramatic creature with a wingspan of 100mm or more and red markings on the abdomen that show as it hovers before flowers, feeding on their nectar. Tiger moths of the family Arctiidae are also poorly represented, with just three native species (*Metacrias* spp.), all with rather similar dark brown and dull yellow markings. There are three common introduced moths: the widespread magpie moth (*Nystemera amica*), which is dark brown with large off-white spots on the wings; the brilliant crimson-coloured cinnabar moth (*Tyria jacobaeae*); and the colourful crimson speckled footman (*Utetheisa pulchelloides*), with its red and black spotted forewings.

FRESHWATER INSECTS

New Zealand's rivers, freshwater lakes and ponds are home to a number of endemic insects, including backswimmers (*Anisops assimilis*), pond skaters (*Microvelia* spp.), the water boatman (*Sigara arguta*) and the unusual water measurer (*Hydrometria risbeci*), which looks rather like a miniature stick insect and which walks quite slowly on the surface of the water. There are also nearly 20 species of water beetle, and they can be found in most parts of the country, even in alpine and warm thermal lakes. The largest is the endemic large diving beetle (*Homeodytes hookeri*) which can be up to 30mm long. In its larval stage it is known as 'water tiger' and both larvae and the adults are hunters of small invertebrates including the larvae of other insects such as mosquitoes as well as small fish and even frogs.

DRAGONFLIES AND DAMSELFLIES

These are among the most easily identifiable insects. There are some 11 native dragonflies, mostly endemic, and they are found from the coast to the alpine regions. Most widespread is the bush giant dragonfly (*Uropetala carovei*). This impressively large and strikingly patterned insect has transparent wings with a span of up to 130mm; the body is dark brown, up to 85mm long, with a banded appearance. It is quite noisy in flight and can consume large numbers of flies and even cicadas. Similar but slightly smaller is the mountain giant dragonfly (*U. chiltoni*) found at higher altitudes. Smaller again and with distinct red colouration is the red percher dragonfly (*Diplacodes bipunctata*), with a wingspan of around 55mm and a body length of 35mm.

The larva or nymphs of dragonflies may spend many years in the pond before developing into adults. They are fearsome predators, striking their prey with powerful thrusts of their extendable lower jaws. When they emerge they break through their old 'skin' and leave it clamped to a plant stem, before taking to the air.

Damselflies are smaller, rather more delicate version of dragonflies. Six species live in New Zealand, with the two commonest being the blue damselfly or kekewai (*Austrolestes colensonis*) and the smaller red damselfly or kihitara (*Xanthocnemis zealandica*). The female kekewai is rather more green than blue. Damselflies have

The bush giant dragonfly is quite noisy; you may see it hunting for small insects. JF

similar life cycles to dragonflies but the nymphs are much smaller; they swim by wiggling and have three tail whiskers. Adults can often be seen linked together in a circle as part of the mating process: the male clasps the female behind the head with his tail claspers, the female then curls her body forward to complete the circle, and the mating.

Other flying insects whose larval stages are underwater are the endemic dobsonfly (*Archicaulioides diversus*), with its short body and very large, long wings, the large green stoneflies (*Stenoperla* spp.) and over 200 species of caddisfly of the order Tricoptera, much appreciated by the trout fishers. Lastly there are the enigmatic mayflies or piriwai, some 40 species of the order Ephereroptera, which may spend up to four years as nymphs before emerging as adults for a whirlwind day or two of mating before they die. As they have no mouth or feeding mechanism they will never last more than a few days and in some cases die within a few hours.

CICADAS

Few sounds can summon up an image of warm summer days like the noise of a cicada. While it may be easier to hear one than to see one, you just need patience. There are some 40 members of the Cicadidae family in New Zealand, all of them endemic. Cicadas are generally commonest in tropical and sub-tropical climes. However, in New Zealand they are found from the coast to the summer snow line, where you may find the high alpine cicada (*Maoricicada nigra*), the smallest of the family, with a body length of 15mm and a wingspan of 30mm, 'singing' its distinctive two-note song. Cicada reproduction is another interesting story. The female cuts a groove in the bark of a tree to lay her eggs. On hatching the larva descends to the ground and burrows into it, living there for three to five years, before emerging to sing, mate and die. One American species has a larval stage lasting 17 years.

The chorus cicada (*Amphipsalta zealandica*), the largest cicada found here, is also the commonest. The wings are always transparent and when folded extend well beyond the end of the abdomen. Its body is attractively patterned in green and black. Others, such as the snoring cicada (*Kikihia cutore*) and the little grass cicada (*K. muta*), have green bodies, while the red-tailed cicada (*Rhodopsalta cruentata*) has just that – with a largely brown head and thorax. Cicadas have two large compound eyes set well apart on their broad blunt heads.

Each species of cicada has its own song, sung only by the males. They make it by vibrating two ribbed membranes or tymbals on the abdomen. The sound is amplified by internal air sacs; the male's

The chorus cicada is endemic and widespread. JF

internal digestive organs are reduced in size to make space for these. When singing, males are not hard to locate, but the silent females most certainly are – both sexes are extremely well camouflaged. Most cicadas sing in the summer and autumn, though a few can be heard year-round.

The common stick insect has two colour forms. TDR

STICK INSECTS

New Zealand has more than 20 endemic species of stick insect, all of which look just like sticks. In all species the female is very much larger than the male, so if you see a large and a small one together, they are probably mating. The largest is the large spiny stick insect (*Argosarchus spiniger*), the female of which can be up to 145mm long. She is grey-brown while the smaller male is a darker blue-grey, and both have small spines on either side of the thorax. Smaller and much commoner is the New Zealand stick insect (*Citarchus hookeri*) the female of which is up to 105mm long. It has two colour forms, a slightly reddish brown and a bright green. One unusual species, the prickly stick insect (*Aconthaxyla prasina*), reproduces parthogenetically, the females producing clones of themselves without needing to mate. In fact no males of this species have ever been identified!

PRAYING MANTIDS

Only two species of this engaging insect group are found here, the endemic New Zealand praying mantis (*Orthodera novaezealandiae*), which is almost entirely green with a pinkish abdomen and a blue and purple patch on the insides of its forelegs, and the introduced African praying mantis (*Miomantis caffra*), which is almost identical but lacks these patches. The African invader is a fairly recent arrival, which is rapidly spreading southwards and may be displacing the native species.

LACEWINGS

These attractive and delicate insects are represented in New Zealand by 16 species, but the one that you are most likely to encounter is the antlion lacewing (*Weeleus acutus*), whose larval stage lives at the bottom of a pit trap, waiting for unsuspecting ants and other wandering invertebrates to tumble in. The adult antlion lacewing looks superficially a bit like a rather small, heavy damselfly, but at rest its transparent wings extend well beyond its abdomen.

The antlion lacewing is easily mistaken for a damselfly. JF

PLANTS AND FUNGI

Cabbage tree or tī kauka TDR

Magnificent, spectacular, amazing, weird or intriguing, virtually all of New Zealand's native plants are endemic. Because of the country's long isolation from Australia and the rest of the world, they have been able to develop in their own ways, in their own very particular climate and geology. The land has grown and shrunk, been submerged, partially covered with ice, experienced massive mountain-building tectonic movements and suffered truly huge volcanic events.

The result of this geological history, all taking place within an oceanic setting, is a great variety of habitats, from coastal wetlands to high alpine fellfields, from dry windswept grasslands to luxuriant rainforests. The forest was the defining feature of the original ecosystem and covered 80% of the country. Thanks to humans and their companions there is now only 25% of that native forest left, but what remains still defines much of the plant life of New Zealand.

Beech forests are especially prevalent in wet or mountainous areas. JF

When you arrive in New Zealand, you will see mainly introduced plants in and around the towns. The native bush was destroyed by the early settlers who brought their own trees, shrubs and other plants, partly for agricultural purposes, partly ornamental and to remind them of home, and partly because wilderness was seen as something to be subdued and changed. Once you leave the urban and the agricultural areas, however, then you will start to see and appreciate the native trees and plants. This chapter focuses on these; they form the natural native ecosystems and are vital to the survival of many native animal species.

TREES AND SHRUBS

There are 260 species of native tree and many more native shrubs, virtually all of them evergreen. Contrast this to only 30 native trees in the British Isles and you will appreciate the richness of the bush. Identifying them is quite a job; the only practical way is to break them down into groups or genera with generally similar characteristics, or habitat.

THE BEECHES

There are four species of beech, one of which has two distinct forms, and they constitute a very distinct forest type, quite different from the podocarp broadleaved forests. Beech forests are quite homogenous and have few other tree species except on the margins. The beeches are all from the genus *Nothofagus* or southern beech. They are all evergreen and have small, rather rounded leaves, no more than 2cm long. Those of the black beech and its mountain form are smooth-margined, while those of hard beech, red beech and silver beech are all toothed. Beeches tend to dominate in cooler, wetter areas and so are most widespread on South Island with red, silver and mountain being found in higher areas with hard and black being found at lower altitudes.

THE CONIFERS

Conifers are the most ancient of trees, having appeared long before flowering plants. Instead of flowers, most of them have male and female cones, the former producing pollen which fertilises the female cones. The seeds develop within the cone and are released when the cone opens. There are 20 species of native conifer, all endemic, and divided into four families; they generally prefer the warmer climes of the North Island but some species are found on all three islands. The largest and most magnificent is the kauri, the sole representative of the Aruacariaceae family, which is found only in the northern half of North Island. A mature kauri with its great column of a trunk soaring into the canopy is a truly awe-inspiring sight; few living things on the planet can match the presence of Tane Mahuta and the slightly smaller Te Matua Ngahere. If you see only one thing when you come to New Zealand, make sure it is these two trees in the Waipoua Forest in Northland.

You can see why kauris were so sought after by the navy to provide spars for sailing ships. JF

The largest group of native conifers, with 14 species, is the Podocarpacidae family or podocarps. Like the kauri, podocarps are tall, very straight emergent trees, and can often be seen protruding through the canopy when viewed from above. One of the most widespread of these is the rimu, quite easily identified by its attractive long, drooping leaves. Rimu, also known as red pine, grows to 35m or more. It, along with the other podocarps, does not produce a multi-seeded cone, but a single seed surrounded by a red fleshy collar at the tip of the branchlets.

The rimu has graceful drooping foliage JF

One podocarp that is often seen 'marooned' individually or in a small clump in a cow pasture is the totara. Often showing a distinctly conical shape, it has rough stringy bark and small narrow leaves, similar to a European yew. Thin-barked or Hall's totara (*Podocarpus. hallii*) is similar but found at higher altitudes and has thin, rich brown papery bark, while the closely related needle-leaved totara (*P. acutifolius*) is a low spreading shrub often found in the forest understorey, particularly in South Island beech forests.

Matai (*Prumnopitys taxifolia*) and miro (*P. ferruginea*) also have small, narrow yew-like leaves, but while matai has blue-black berries and white undersides to the leaves, miro has red berries and the undersides of its leaves are green. Lastly there is the kahikatea or white pine. This tall, elegant, moisture-loving tree is found on the edges of swamps, ponds and lakes. It has a distinctive twisting trunk, buttress roots and a clearly conical overall shape.

The two other conifer families are the Phylocladaceae or celery pines, and the Cupresaceae or cypresses. The former is represented by three species: tanekaha (*Phyllocladus trichomanoides*), toatoa (*P. toatoa*) and mountain toatoa (*P. asplenifolius*), whose celery-like leaves are actually flattened branchlets. There are two species of cypress: kawaka (*Libocedrus plumosa*) and kaikawaka

Podocarp/broadleaf forest is very varied. TDR

Tall podocarps tower over the tree ferns and stick up through the canopy. JF

The forest floor is rich in fungi, fern fronds and seedlings. TDR

In full bloom the kanuka turns white. TDR

The seeds of kahikatea have bright red fleshy covers to attract birds. JF

(*L. bidwilli*), both of which are widespread. They grow to 25m and have a distinct conical shape. The leaves of kawaka are flattened and have a weeping appearance, while kaikawaka has thin twig-like leaves.

KAURI

The kauri trees of northern North Island are among the largest living organisms on the planet. Tane Mahuta, the largest known individual, has a trunk diameter of 4.4m, which it retains throughout a trunk height of nearly 18m, a volume of nearly 250m³. On top is a huge, epiphyte-filled crown. It is reckoned to be about 2,000 years old. Te Matua Ngahere is shorter but broader, with a trunk diameter of 5.2m, but a volume of nearer 200m³.

Kauri survived the arrival of the Maori – not having steel they were unable to fell the large ones. For Europeans they were a dream come true, tall and straight with a very clean grain. The wood was easily worked and was ideal for ship masts and hulls. They were felled in large numbers, often very wastefully. Thankfully, kauris are now largely protected and in many areas in Northland and the Coromandel, you can see large numbers of 'rickers' as the young trees are called, growing together with impressively straight trunks.

Logging kauris is hard work, very wasteful and requires a team of men. ATL/Northwood Collections

The secret of the very clean-grained wood is that the lower branches are pushed out of the trunk as the tree grows, leaving no knots. Only when a crown develops do the branches remain attached to the tree for long periods. The trunks themselves have a diagnostic pattern as the bark flakes off in large rounded scabs leaving a smooth and yet undulating surface, with recently exposed areas being quite pink, older exposed areas greyer. Fallen kauris that had been preserved in swamps for hundreds of years were hauled out once the technology existed to do so and the wood was found to be as good as ever.

Kauri gum, which is exuded by the tree, was also highly prized. It was used by the Maoris who chewed it and used its soot for tattooing, and by the Europeans for paint, varnish and linoleum. Semi-fossilised gum has also been found in the swamps.

BROADLEAF CANOPY TREES

These are all evergreen flowering trees, which co-exist with the conifers. New Zealand forests are temperate rainforests, and while they do not have the huge range of species found in tropical rainforests, they do have far more than their northern counterparts. One of the most widespread families here is the ratas, members of the Myrtaceae family. They come in three forms: trees, shrubs and vines. The northern rata (*Metrosideros robusta*) starts life as an epiphyte, developing in the crown of a large rimu or similar podocarp. Once established it sends down roots which over the years grow, coalesce and envelop the trunk of the host tree. The host then dies, its demise probably hastened by the rata, and leaves the rata standing in its place, often with a hollow trunk near the base. The southern rata (*M. umbellata*) is similar in appearance but rather smaller and only rarely grows as an epiphyte. Both produce a profusion of scarlet, feathery flowers which turn the whole tree red.

Similarly endowed with magnificent red flowers is the pohutakawa, a large, spreading tree that can grow to 20m or more. It particularly likes coastal areas and you'll find them growing right up to the shoreline, often leaning out over the water. Pohutakawa is sometimes referred to as the New Zealand Christmas tree as it flowers at that time of the year. It is naturally confined to North Island but has been planted as far south as Christchurch. It has survived better than most natives because of its ability to grow on cliffs and similar places, inaccessible to grazing and browsing mammals.

Another widespread lowland species is the puriri, which lives to a great age and spreads out as its branches root. These trees often become hollow and were used by the Maori as burial trees. They produce dark red flowers in winter which attract many native bird species. They also host the caterpillars of the large puriri moth. The wood is very hard and durable and was used for railway sleepers.

Two trees belonging to the laurel family are important canopy trees: tawa (*Beilschmiedia tawa*) is found mainly in North Island and the top of South Island, while the related taraire (*B. tarairi*) is found further south. Tawa has narrow drooping willow-like leaves while taraire has broad glossy green ones. You may see the kereru or New Zealand pigeon enjoying the large fruit of either of these trees.

Rewarewa (*Knightia excelsa*) is a tree that often grows close to old Maori settlements or pas, and has a tall, almost cylindrical shape. The flowers are large and somewhat brush-like, and it produces huge amounts of yellow fruit, rather like small dates. These were a

Southern rata turns crimson when in flower. JF

127

favourite food for Maori, which accounts for the trees' presence in Maori areas; the fruits are also favoured by the kereru.

One of the most widespread trees is kamahi, found throughout the country, especially in montane forests; it produces huge numbers of pinkish finger-like inflorescences in the spring. From Auckland northwards it is replaced by towai (*Weinmannia silvicola*), which has white inflorescences (flower clusters). Also found in lowland and montane forest is broadleaf or kapuka, which has large, oval, glossy green leaves with yellow stems. Somewhat smaller and lower down is puka or shining broadleaf (*Griselinia lucida*), whose leaves are a bright glossy green and asymmetrical at the base. Puka is most often an epiphyte but can grow terrestrially as well.

top The unusual, brush-like flowers of rewarewa. JF
left The candle-shaped inflorescences of kamahi completely cover the tree. JF

TREE BARKS

Many of the larger trees, especially the podocarps, are best identified by their bark, as very often that is the only part you can see as the large straight trunk vanishes through the canopy. These trees employ a variety of strategies to stop mosses, vines and other epiphytes from growing on their trunks, and this is evident from their bark. Kauri and matai drop large flakes, the latter leaving chestnut-brown scars, while rimu and kawaka shed long strips of bark, as do kanuka and tree fuchsia. Totara has thick stringy bark that sheds steadily, as does that of mountain totara though it is thin and papery.

The patterns left by flaking kauri bark can be works of art. JF

SMALLER TREES AND SHRUBS

The lowland and montane forests are well endowed with small trees and shrubs, which you'll notice as the next layer down from the canopy – the sub-canopy. One of the commonest is mahoe (*Melicytus ramiflorus*), known in English as whiteywood. This is a small, fast-growing tree of the forest edge. Its leaves are toothed and the flower clusters, with greenish-white flowers, grow straight out of the branches and produce purple berries later on. Its wood is very light and dries quickly; Maori used it to start fires. Pigeonwood or porokaiwhiri (*Hedycara arborea*) is slightly larger, with gently toothed leaves which have reddish midribs; its bright red fruit are another kereru favourite.

Several small trees or shrubs have distinctive leaves. Marbleleaf or putaputaweta (*Carpodetus serratus*) has two forms: a juvenile divaricating form, with very small almost round serrated leaves, and an adult form with much longer leaves. Kaikomako (*Pennantia corymbosa*) is similar in having two forms; its leaves are more lobed but are similarly almost round in the divaricating juvenile stage and much larger and longer in the adult stage. Other species that have very distinctive leaves are five-finger or whauwhaupaku (*Pseudopanax arboreus*), which produces clusters of dark flowers in the spring that turn into large bunches of small black fruit in the autumn, and pate or seven finger (*Schefflera digitata*), which often has up to ten 'fingers' on its leaves. Wineberry or makomako (*Aristotelia serrata*) has large toothed leavers and produces a profusion of small berries that turn from green to red to black. Kawakawa (*Libocedrus plumosa*) has large, almost heart-shaped leaves, nearly always with holes in them caused by a native moth caterpillar, which never eats the whole leaf, just bits of all of them. The stems are jointed, rather like bamboo, and the flower spike is a small upright candle that turns bright orange when the fruit ripens.

Among the very few deciduous trees are the kowhai and the tree fuchsia or kotukutuku. Kowhai is not endemic, being found in southern Chile and, remarkably, on Gough Island in the South Atlantic. It has spread to these diverse locations thanks to its very hard seeds, which are able to stand long periods immersed in seawater. Kowhai produces a profusion of bright yellow tubular flowers in the early spring and is a big favourite with the tui. The leaves appear after the flowering. Similarly, the tree fuchsia produces its distinctive purplish, bell-shaped flowers before the leaves grow directly off the trunk or branch. A rather untidy spreading tree, it can be identified

The flowers of mahoe or whiteywood grow directly on the branchlets. TDR

by its constantly peeling reddish-brown bark. A shrub with a very distinctive flower, in this case red, is the kakabeak or kowhai ngutu-kaka (*Clianthus maximus*). A rather sprawling shrub, it produces large scarlet flowers shaped like the curved bill of a kaka.

Another distinctive shrub is tutu (*Coriaria arborea*). A rather messy plant, it is an early coloniser of waste or open ground. It produces tall spikes or branches with opposite leaves, which encircle or wrap around the branch. The flowers are small and white and hang down in long racemes which may be 20cm long. The flowers turn into dark purple berries in due course. Both the plant and the fruit are poisonous.

Five-finger or whauwhaupaku, with its distinctive large black fruiting umbels. JF

Coprosmas – the coffee family

Coprosma means 'smelling like dung', a rather off-putting name for this group of shrubs and small trees related to the coffee plant. There are more than 50 species of coprosma in New Zealand. Most are shrubs but eight species grow into small trees. The stinkwood (*Coprosma grandifolia*) can be identified by the rotten-egg smell which is released if you crush its leaves or stems – if you really want to experience it! The leaves are generally oval, opposite, often pointed and smooth-margined, and the flowers are pale greenish-yellow. All members of this genus use the wind to distribute their pollen. The male flowers have long stamens and the females long (sometimes very long) stigma, like tongues sticking out to catch passing pollen grains. The fruits are small fleshy berries containing two seeds, just like a coffee bean; in fact you can make 'coffee' from them, but as they are so small you'll need a lot of them. The berries are nearly always shiny and vary from translucent white to blue, yellow, orange and red. They are often produced in large bunches, particularly on karamu (*C. robusta*) and shining karamu (*C. lucida*). Both are widespread but karamu prefers wetter habitats than shining karamu. Taupata is a common coprosma shrub along the coast – you'll often find it right on the beach. It has large, dark green, distinctly veined and shiny leaves. Kanono (*C. grandifolia*) is also widespread and produces large quantities of berries, but its leaves are not glossy and are slightly marbled or mottled.

DIVARICATING SHRUBS

'Divaricating' is a botanical term describing a plant whose shoots or branches diverge from the main shoot at right angles or obtuse angles. In other words, the shrub grows back into itself and creates a thoroughly tangled mass of twigs and branches, often quite impenetrable, especially in older plants at higher altitudes. Why, we do not know for certain, but it seems likely that this strategy protected the plant from being damaged by grazing birds such as the moas. The great grazing birds are long gone, but the divaricating strategy remains quite effective against sheep, goats and other introduced mammalian herbivores.

The Pittosporums

This is another well-represented genus (*Pittosporum*) of small bushy trees and shrubs, with 26 species found from the coast to alpine regions, including a number that are divaricating shrubs (see box above). The leaves are generally quite long, oval, smooth-margined and alternate, very often with a prominent pale midrib. In the divaricating shrub species such as *P. divaricatum*, a lowland forest species, and *P. rigidum*, a montane forest species, the leaves are small and varied, being either lobed or slightly toothed. The flower buds have scales and the flowers are five-petalled with the petals curving backwards. The fruit are black and sticky and are held in a woody capsule that splits open when mature.

Pittosporum tenuifolium has the turned back petals typical of its genus. JF

Common species are tarata or lemonwood (*P. eugeniodes*), which has yellow flowers, and yellowish-green leaves with undulating margins, and a strong scent of lemon when crushed. Karo has bright red flowers and rather thick leaves that are white and furry on the underside. In contrast, kohuhu (*P. tenuifolium*) is a tree up to 8m high and has dark purple to black flowers growing singly from the branches. Another species, *P. colensoi*, is similar but is found at higher altitudes, while *P. ralphii* has rich crimson flowers and is found south as far as Hawkes Bay.

Tree daisies

One of the interesting aspects of the ecology of oceanic islands is that a single species, once it's managed to get there, will often diversify and develop into many different species. The genera *Olearia* and *Brachyglottis* are two such groups that each probably evolved from a single ancestor. These tree daisies have composite flowers, the central part of the flower being composed of many, often hundreds, much smaller, mini flowers. There are over 40 species or subspecies of *Olearia*, which have

The common tree daisy is one of many similar species found in New Zealand. JF

white outer petals, and more than 30 of *Brachyglottis*, which have either yellow or white outer petals. The name *Brachyglottis* translates as 'short-tongued', referring to the shortness of the petals in the centre of the flower.

Tree daisies are commonest at higher altitudes and along forest margins. They are widespread and when in flower can't be mistaken for anything else. The common tree daisy (*O. arborescens*) has large sprays of daisy-like flowers. Its thick, coarsely toothed leaves are on long stalks and are grey-green underneath. Akeake (*O. avicennifolia*) has only a few outer petals, long pointed leaves and very papery peeling bark, while the leaves of tanguru (*O. furfuracea*) have buff-coloured hairs on the undersides. The trunk has rough and peeling bark. The commonest member of the *Brachyglottis* genus is probably rangiora (*B. repanda*) which produces a profusion of small pale-yellow flowers. Also widespread on North Island is *B. rotundifolia*, which has leathery leaves and no outer petals on the flowers.

The cord-like branches of the whipcord hebes have their leaves pressed close to the stem. TDR

Hebes

The genus *Hebe* is the largest plant genus in New Zealand, with over 90 species or subspecies, all of them endemic. Hebes are popular garden shrubs worldwide, and gardeners have produced many new varieties. You can find examples of the group in all habitats apart from dense forest; they are particularly well represented in coastal and alpine areas. One of the commonest lowland species is willow-leaved hebe (*H. salicifolia*), with long, narrow, pointed leaves and large, drooping, white flower clusters. Several similar species including koromiko (*H. stricta*), *H. linguistifiolia* and *H. acutiflora* have rather shorter leaves, and smaller, mauve inflorescences. The largest is the tree hebe (*H. parviflora*) which can grow to over 7m high; it sometimes forms dense clumps. The flowers appear on short spikes at the branch tips, sometimes completely covering the tree with blossom.

PALMS, CABBAGES AND GRASS TREES

This is a disparate collection of smaller trees, grouped together because they are all rather bizarre.

Palms

There is just one species of native palm, the nikau palm (*Rhopalostylis sapida*). It is the world's most cold-tolerant palm species and is found as far south as the Banks Peninsula and Okarito. It grows to 15m or more and you're unlikely to confuse it with anything other than a tree fern. Its smooth, ringed trunk, bulbous base to the crown, long single pinnate fronds and large hanging inflorescences growing directly out of the trunk make it easy to identify.

Nikau palm is the most southerly species of palm. TDR

Cabbage trees

The ti kauka or cabbage tree (see page 121) is one of those slightly surreal-looking plants that makes you wonder 'Why?' They come straight out of a Dr Seuss book. Cabbage trees are found throughout the country up to about 1,000m, but are especially fond of wetlands. It seems to produce a huge inflorescence of creamy-white flowers in the spring and purplish-white berries later on. You will see them in cow or sheep pastures, standing alone or in small isolated groups, a clear sign of drainage or other 'land improvement'. You can check out this species in some places before you travel to New Zealand – including Park Lane in London and Torbay in Devon.

The cabbage tree produces large white inflorescences. TDR

Two related species are the forest cabbage tree (*C. banksii*) and the mountain cabbage tree. The former is smaller, generally unbranched and has a fan or fountain-like foliage arrangement. It also has a very large white inflorescence, up to 150cm long. The mountain cabbage tree is similar but has much larger and broader leaves with a skirt of dead ones obscuring its trunk. You will only find it in montane forest, especially along the margins. It has a similar enormous inflorescence, with densely packed white flowers on individual fingers.

The very broad, pointed leaves of the mountain cabbage tree are diagnostic. JF

Grass trees (Dracophyllums)

You might think the grass or pineapple trees look like miniature cabbage trees. They are all members of the genus *Dracophyllum*, which is part of the Ericaceae, or heather family. The 35 endemic species or subspecies of grass tree found in New Zealand occur in all but wetland habitats, with many found in alpine and sub-alpine

Dracophyllums are typical shrubs of higher altitudes. JF

regions. The largest is the mountain neinei (*D. traversii*), which can be over 10m tall, with large, pineapple-shaped bunches of leaves and big red conical inflorescences. Much smaller is the small bushy totorowhiti (*D. strictum*), which is only 2m tall and has white inflorescences. Another lowland or montane species is the slender-stemmed neinei (*D. latifolium*), which has much finer leaves. It is shorter than the mountain neinei and has a very thin trunk, giving it a slightly ungainly appearance.

ALPINE TREES AND SHRUBS

The alpine regions of New Zealand include some of the country's least damaged habitats. Even here the ecosystem is not pristine, thanks to the presence of alien weed species and ungulates such as goats, thar and chamois, but nevertheless the native flora is large and varied. While most alpine plants are herbaceous, there are a surprising number of alpine and sub-alpine shrubs, some of which you have to examine very closely to see if they are woody or herbaceous.

Alpine buttercups. MJ

Many of the alpine shrubs belong to genera or families that we have already seen at lower altitudes. This is particularly so of the grass tree genus *Dracophyllum* and the hebes, but also includes coprosmas, pittosporums, tree daisies of the genera Olearia and Brachyglottis, and conifers such as snow totara (*Podocarpus nivalis*), mountain pine (*Dacrydium bidwillii*) and the pygmy pine (*D. laxifolium*), which is the smallest conifer in the world, a low-spreading shrub that rarely reaches 75cm in height.

The Dracophyllums are well represented, with more than 15 species, two of which, monoao (*D. subulatum*) and *D. filifolium*, grow to about 2m and have long upward-pointing needle-like leaves and small white bell-shaped flowers. Similar but smaller and with much shorter leaves is the turpentine scrub (*D. uniflorum*). Hebes are also here in numbers with over 30 species. They are best characterised by two distinct types. The whipcord hebes such as *H. lycopodioides* on South Island and *H. tetragona* on North Island have their leaves flattened onto their branches, giving them the appearance of pipe cleaners. In contrast *H. canterburiensis* and *H. odora* have short, stiff, very regular opposite leaves, arranged on alternate sides of the stem in a very compact and neat arrangement. Both groups have white flowers that appear in small bunches at the tips of the branches.

You are more likely to find tree daisies in the sub-alpine areas. The holly-leaved tree daisy (*O. ilicifolia*) is very distinctive, with prickly-looking leaves, while the mountain tree daisy (*Brachyglottis bidwillii*) has no petals on its flowers and dark furry undersides to its leaves. A species with thick, heavily serrated leaves is tupare (*O. colensoi*); this is widespread and found in sub-alpine areas on all three main islands and to sea level on Stewart Island.

There are several ground-hugging shrubs. *Pentachondra pumila* is notable for its small white flowers and bright red berries – often both present at the same time on the same plant. Very similar but with white undersides to the leaves is *Cyathodes pumila*. Neither of these two shrubs is more than 4cm high. Several species of coprosma also form very low, creeping shrubs, including *C. petriei*, with white berries and *C. atropurpurea*, with red berries. Slightly taller is *C. brunnea*, which has blue berries.

MANGROVES

Although this group of trees is normally associated with tropical zones, one species of mangrove – *Avicennia marina* – is found in northern North Island as far south as Ohiwa Harbour in the Bay of Plenty. Mangroves are important shore stabilisers and provide sea defence as well as forming a significant ecosystem of their own. Their root systems provide an important habitat for a number of crustaceans, as well as being a breeding ground and nursery for several species of fish. In the far north they can grow to 15m, but at the southern limit of their range they are small shrubs no more than 1m high. Interestingly mangroves have been expanding in area, much to the consternation of shore-dwellers losing their view. This is partly due to the large amount of silt in many rivers due to poor agricultural and forestry practices. Sometime the natives strike back!

The native mangrove is wonderfully adapted to its habitat. JF

HERBACEOUS PLANTS

As you would expect, given its wide range of habitats, New Zealand has a great variety of herbaceous plants. These plants are distinct from the shrubs and trees in that their stems and leaves last for only one year or one growing season. As with the other plant groups, the large majority of the native species are endemic. Most of the herbaceous plants that you see in urban and agricultural areas are introduced; many will already be familiar to the European or North American visitor. If you recognise it, it is probably an alien!

COASTAL AND WETLAND HERBS

North Island boasts a number of large harbours or estuaries and their associated wetlands, sadly much diminished from their original size. Here you can see a variety of plants that are adapted to this often harsh, salty environment – many of them being important and integral parts of coastal defences. Seagrass (*Zostera capricornia*) is able to survive below the low tide line and helps to anchor sediments. It is in serious decline, most likely due to pollution. Another species, saltwort (*Sarcocornia*

Native iceplant or horokak. JF

quinqueflora) grows in dense stands in estuaries around the high-tide mark. It is a succulent (fleshy) plant with greyish-green or reddish stems, which look like pipe cleaners.

On the beach and rocks above the high-tide line you may come across a couple of quite small umbellifers. They are Lyall's carrot (*Anisotme lyallii*), with almost fern-like leaves and large flower heads, and Maori celery (*Apium prostratum*), which is smaller and sprawling with much smaller flower heads. Several members of the daisy family also like coastal habitats, including shore groundsel (*Senecio lautus*), with its slightly fleshy leaves and round yellow flowers, which look as though someone has been pulling the outer petals off a daisy to leave just the centre; and yellow woollyhead (*Craspedia uniflora*) and buttonweed (*Leptinella coronopifolia*), which have yellow pincushion-like flowers. The buttonweed has much smaller and more numerous flowers than the woollyhead, and bears them on shorter stems. Another common plant is the spreading succulent horokaka or native ice plant (*Disphyma australe*) with its large, rather ostentatious, pinkish-purple flowers; the leaves are peg-like and often reddish in colour. Also with pink flowers, though in this case they are pink and white striped, is the shore bindweed (*Calystegia soldanella*).

One much smaller plant, especially in damp areas behind sand dunes, is sand gunnera *Gunnera arenaria*. It has dark greenish-purple leaves and forms low patches; the small white flowers are on small spikes turning to globular orange coloured fruit. Its close relative *G. preorepens* has red fruit. Both are relatives of the huge introduced, Chilean rhubarb *G. tinctoria*. Also common are two species of beach spinach, *Tetragonia tetragonioides* and *T. implexicoma*, both of which are edible and have very small yellow flowers. On rocky shorelines you may see the native plantain *Plantago raoulii*, with its flat rosette of deeply indented leaves and numerous flower spikes that grow outwards and then upwards.

HERBACEOUS PLANTS OF THE FORESTS

Parataniwha prefers very shady areas. JF

Dense forest is not the ideal place for small terrestrial herbs, but even so there are quite a few – especially on the margins. One notable species is parataniwha (*Elastostema rugosum*), a spreading leafy perennial with greenish-purple leaves that forms dense patches; the flowers are small and inconspicuous. Two daisies found in the forests are the profuse hanging daisy (*Anaphalioides trinervis*) often seen on banks and cuttings, and the much smaller (and less pronounceable) papataniwhaniwha (*Lagenifera petiolata*), which grows in small patches on banks or beside trails. An unusual small herb is *Pratia angulata*, with its white

Onion-leaved orchid. JF

lopsided flowers and small dull-red berries. If you spot small bright orange berries, they probably belong to one of several species of *Nertera*: small mat-forming relatives of the coprosmas. The endemic *N. depressa* and the native *N. cunninghamii* have smooth leaves, while *N. dichrondiofolia*, *N. villosa* and *N. cillata* are all hairy. Hairiness is also the defining characteristic of the hairy buttercup (*Ranunculus reflex*), a small forest plant with very small yellow buttercup-like flowers. Also adapted to life in the forest are two species of oxalis: white oxalis (*O. magellanica*) and creeping oxalis (*O. exilis*). The latter has yellow flowers, and both have typical rather clover-like three-lobed leaves. Rauhia or linen flax (*Linum monoganum*) has quite large, upwards-pointing white flowers at the tips of its stems, while akapohue or pink bindweed (*Calystegia sepium*) has large pink flowers and behaves like all bindweeds, scrambling up and over other plants and sometimes swamping them in the process.

There are a considerable number of orchids in New Zealand. Many of them are epiphytic and grow at the tops of large podocarps, but you may find several species such as maikuku or small sun orchid (*Thelymitra longifolia*) growing on the ground in large colonies. The maikuku has a white flower and a leaf that curves away from the stem halfway up. There are some 12 species in the same genus, with *T. colensoi* and the blue sun orchid (*T. pauciflora*) both having attractive blue or mauve-blue flowers.

GRASSES AND OTHER TUFTED PLANTS

There are nearly 200 species of native grasses in New Zealand. Most of them grow near the coast, in the tussock grasslands of South Island or in the alpine areas. However, some species are found in the bush, notably the bush rice grass (*Microlaena avenacea*) with its graceful, drooping flower spikes, and the large hunangamoho (*Chionochloa conspicua*), with its tussock-like form and profusion of flower heads. Watch out also for hookgrasses (*Uncina* spp.): small tussocky grasses with seeds that easily attach themselves to you. One tufted species that is a member of the lily family rather than a grass is kakaha (*Astelia fragrans*), which has graceful drooping, silvery-green leaves that can be up to 150cm long. It has a large drooping inflorescence that gives off a sweet scent; the fruit is an orange berry in a yellow cup.

You'll certainly notice the native pampas grass or toetoe (*Cortaderia fulvida*). This tall grass is unmistakeable, especially in late summer and autumn when it produces flower spikes up to 4m tall. It is common on North Island. Another distinctive tufted plant is harakeke or New Zealand flax (*Phormium tenax*), which has very large broad flat leaves 2m or more long. The oddly shaped flowers grow in bunches on a very tall flower spike and provide an important source of nectar for birds in the spring.

On sand dunes there are three native grasses, which help to stabilise the sand. Sand tussock (*Austrofestuca littoralis*) is a tall, upright, tufted yellowish grass, while both pingao and spinifex or kowhangatara are shorter but propagate with long creeping rhizomes (underground stems) as well as by seeds. All three species are dominant but do not exclude other species. This is not the case with the introduced marram grass *Ammopohila arenaria*, which will completely take over a dune system.

A widespread saltmarsh grass is sea rush (*Juncus kraussii*). It often grows in dense stands, and you'll also see it around thermal springs near Rotorua and elsewhere inland away from the influence of salt water. Raupo or bulrush (*Typha orientalis*) is common, often in drainage ditches and beside streams; its large, dark brown,

Tussock grasslands cover large areas of upland. TDR

tubular seed heads are unmistakable. New Zealand also has many species of sedge and cutty grass, including purei (*Carex secta*), which can develop a large stool, and broad-leaved sedge (*Machaerina sinclairii*), with tall drooping leaves and dark brown flowerheads. Giant sedge (*Ghania xathocarpa*) is one of the largest and is a forest plant, while coastal cutty grass (*Cyperus ustulatus*) is found close to the coast, especially in wetlands.

In drier areas on South Island, and in alpine and sub-alpine areas, the dominant grasses are the tussock grasses, which often cover large areas. Most noticeable are the snow tussocks of the genus *Chinochloa* as well as hard tussock (*Festuca novae-zelandia*) and silver tussock (*Poa cita*). One that you will also see out of its native habitat is red tussock, as it is much favoured by landscapers and appears in town parks and by road junctions. In alpine and sub-alpine areas the tallest plants are often the flower spikes of some of the 39 species of endemic speargrasses or spaniards (*Aciphylla* spp.). These have stiff tufted leaves and a very large, often 3m-tall flower spike. Some are also armed with fearsome spines. These formidable plants go by suitably threatening names such as 'fierce', 'wild' or 'horrid'. They are also found in lowland areas but are more common higher up.

Speargrasses or spaniards have tall flower spikes. TDR

from top to bottom Bulbinellas in spring;
brown mountain daisy; South Island edelweiss;
ourisia and mountain buttercup. TDR

ALPINE AND SUB-ALPINE HERBACEOUS PLANTS

Tramping in the alpine areas of New Zealand is a popular pastime, with most people coming to enjoy the wonderful views and the sense of freedom, but the real glory of the alpine regions is the flora. This is the richest area for plants, and especially herbs, with well over 50% of all herb species found here. Alpine plants tend to grow, flower and fruit quite quickly as their growing season is that much shorter than in lowland areas. The beginning of the flowering season varies with altitude and latitude so that in North Island some species start flowering in October while further south they may not start until December. Most flowering is over by late February or March. Some 77% of the New Zealand alpines have white flowers – nearly double the world average. This may be linked to the lack of specialised insect pollinators in the alpine habitat. A white, bowl-shaped flower is a good general design which will attract unspecialised pollinators, and – as generating coloured flowers takes up more of the plant's resources – why waste energy?

Here again certain families have done particularly well. The largest single family is the daisies with more than 30 species represented here, varying from the small matt daisies such as *Celmisia sessiflora* or *C. argentea*, which hug the ground, to the large *C. semicordata* whose flower stems can be 60cm high, or the brown mountain daisy (*C. traversii*), the underside of whose leaves are covered with rich brown fur. Most remarkable are the vegetable sheep (*Raoulia* spp.), which from a distance look like white rocks but are in

140

fact boulder-shaped members of the daisy family, with hundreds of small plantlets gradually growing outwards. They are extremely well adapted to the harsh alpine conditions. Among the most attractive alpine flowers are the edelweisses. The two species, north and south, are similar in appearance with a white star-shaped flower, and are not in fact related to the European edelweiss.

Alpine gentians in full bloom. TDR

Buttercups are also well represented, with at least 17 species, including the largest in the world, the Mount Cook lily, which can grow to a height of 150cm and has large cup-shaped white flowers. Most of the other species, such as korikori (*R. insignis*), have yellow flowers. There are several species of gentian in the alpine areas. The common or small snow gentian (*Gentiana bellidifolia*) is widespread and has typically upwards-pointing sprays of white flowers and dark glossy green leaves, often with a deep red or bronze

Snow gentian: found in most alpine areas. JF

tinge. Quite similar but found only in South Island is the snow gentian (*G. corymbifera*), which produces a profusion of flowers in closely packed umbels; the petals are often veined with purple. A widespread member of the carrot family is the New Zealand angelica (*Gingidia montana*), with generous white-flowered sprays and delicate pinnate leaves. Also widespread are eyebright (*Euphrasia revoluta*), a small grassland plant with delicate yellow-throated flowers, and alpine cushion (*Donatia novae-zelandia*), with its mass of white, pointy-petalled flowers embedded in the dense cushion of succulent green leaves. Other widespread white-flowered species are alpine forget-me-not (*Myosotis suavis*), mountain foxglove (*Ourisia macrocarpa*), and alpine avens (*Geum uniflorum*), a prostrate plant with dark green to purple, very rounded leaves, which forms large patches. Less common is the unusual penwiper (*Notothlaspi rosulatum*), with its rosette of overlapping leaves and densely flowered stubby, central inflorescence. This is one of a number of specialised plants, including scree epilobium (*Epilobium picnostachyum*) that grow only on loose scree slopes.

Still with the white flowers, keep an eye open for the New Zealand violet (*Viola cunninghamii*), panekenake (*Pratia angulata*), with its attractive lop-sided flowers and the onion orchid (*Mictrotis unifolia*), one of several modest alpine orchids. Try and avoid bidibidi (*Acaena anserifolia*), a widespread scrambling plant with globular flower heads: it produces a profusion of barbed seeds that can spell ruination to a pair of socks. Much smaller are two species of insectivorous sundews: *Drosera spathula*, with long, almost rectangular leaves covered with sticky hairs, and *D. stenopetala*, which is similar but with spoon-shaped leaves.

Coloured flowers are much less common. Most spectacular are the bulbinellas (*Bulbinella* spp.), which are like a small yellow version of the red hot poker plant you may have in your garden. Bulbinellas appear in profusion in alpine meadows in the spring. Most of the buttercups (*Ranunculus* spp.) have yellow flowers, as do two members of the daisy family, including the yellow snow marguerite (*Dolichoglottis lyalli*) and the scree groundsel (*Senecio galaucophyllus*). Some of the vegetable sheep have red or yellow flowers, while two plants with large tufted leaves, mountain astelia (*Astelia nervosa*) and mountain flax (*Phormium cookianum*), have greenish-yellow and orange-red flowers respectively, both on large flowerspikes. There are two widespread blue-flowered plants, both with small, slim-stemmed rather delicate flowers. They are rimu-roa (*Wahlenbergia violacea*) and New Zealand harebell (*W. albomarginata*). The latter often has violet-coloured veins and is found only in the higher regions, while rimu-roa is more widespread and is often almost white.

VINES, EPIPHYTES AND PARASITES

Given the extent of the original forest ecosystem, it is not surprising that New Zealand has a wealth of specialised plants that make use of other plants to enjoy their own particular lifestyle. Vines wrap themselves around existing vegetation to avoid having to support themselves: much less effort if someone else will do it for you. Epiphytes avoid the need to struggle up through the canopy by simply starting off up there. Parasites do both and use their host's larder at the same time.

Supplejack creates amazing tangles of stems in the bush. JF

VINES

New Zealand's vines include the extraordinary ratas (*Metrosideros* spp.), of which six species are true vines, starting off on the ground and ending up with massive cable-like stems supported by the host tree. As with the tree ratas described above, most of them have crimson flowers but *M. perforata* (which can often be seen in its very early stages, feeling its way gingerly up a rimu trunk), has white flowers. So do *M. diffusa* and *M. colensoi*, though both of these have a pinkish tinge. At the other end of the scale are the small wiry climbers like bush lawyer or tataramoa, which you will know all about if it gets its downcurved hooks into you or your clothing. It produces large bunches of pinkish-white flowers and, as a member of the blackberry family, has similar-looking fruit. A close relative, *Rubus squarrosus*, has a juvenile form that looks like a tangle of wire, as the leaves have no blades, just a midrib. The leaf form becomes more conventional when the plant matures and reaches the canopy.

A widespread, rather larger vine is supplejack or kareao (*Ripogonum scandens*), which is prolific and can produce an amazing impenetrable tangle of 10–20mm-diameter black stems, often with no sign of the almost oval opposite leaves or the bright orange red berries, which are up in the canopy. For beauty it is hard to beat the native clematis or puawhananga (*Clematis paniculata*) with its mass of delicate, almost dreamy white flowers, while *C. foetida* produces a mass of creamy yellow flowers. Both species have the distinctive hairy seedheads, rather similar to the noxious weed traveller's

Few flowers can match the beauty of the New Zealand clematis. TDR

joy (*C. vitalba*). Another distinctive climber is kiekie (*Freycinetia banksii*), which produces large tussocks of grass-like leaves from a thick vine; it often entirely obscures the trunk of the tree on which it is growing. At the smaller end of the scale are a number of climbing ferns, two of which are mentioned in the fern section. My favourite is mangemange (*Lygodium articulatum*), which has very different fronds – some fertile and some sterile. The latter are like pairs of simple strap leaves, while the fertile ones are almost hand-shaped, with many lobes.

EPIPHYTES

With its wealth of large trees, copious rainfall and mild temperatures, New Zealand is epiphyte heaven. Epiphytes simply sit on other plants, or even rocks, in order to get sunlight. As they cannot obtain water from the ground they need quite specialised systems to deal with periods of drought, though some, such as the two small shrubs *Pittosporum cornifolium* and puka (*Griselinia lucida*), do send down roots to the forest floor. Among the most impressive 'plants in the sky' are the nest epiphytes, such as kowharawhara (*Astelia solandri*), a member of the lily family. It has a fan-shaped spray of long broad leaves, which festoon the tree and look like large birds' nests. They can become so heavy that the supporting branches break off – sometimes the whole tree comes down. Orchids are well represented among the epiphytes, with seven species. The attractive white-flowered *Earina autumnalis* is quite common, as is the yellow- and green-flowered *E. mucronata*. Several species of shrub are also epiphytic and contribute to the veritable gardens, mini ecosystems in their own right, that grow in the treetops – especially in the crowns of the massive kauri trees.

PARASITES

These climbing plants tap into the roots or stems of their hosts and hijack their resources. New Zealand really goes to town with its one parasitic group – the mistletoes. The country has at least nine species from six separate genera. All the species are endemic as are five of the genera. The sight of *Peraxilla tetrapetala* or *P. colensoi* in full flower is quite spectacular: they produce a mass of bright orange-red flowers, which are much loved by tuis, bellbirds and other nectar-feeders. Sadly, several species are threatened by possums and have been protected in places by wire netting. Mistletoes are the only parasitic plants here, though having green leaves does mean that they do provide some of their own food through photosynthesis.

Native mistletoe is seriously threatened by possums. TDR

FERNS AND OTHER SIMPLE PLANTS

The simpler plants aren't always as eye-catching as their relatives, for they lack flowers and many of them are small and discreet. However, take a closer look and you'll appreciate their special beauty and, often, their sheer otherworldliness.

FERNS

Ferns are ancient and most unusual plants. They do not produce flowers and have a two-stage reproductive process whereby the spores produced by the mature plant germinate into 'gametophytes', which produce eggs and sperm cells. Once fertilised, the egg cells grow into the sporophyte or spore-producing plants – what you will recognise as the actual fern.

Most obvious and impossible to miss are the tree ferns. There are nine species from two genera:

Tree ferns are characteristic of the New Zealand bush. TDR

Dicksonia and *Cyathea*. The tree ferns are an important component of the forest ecosystem, with their amazing fibrous trunks and graceful drooping fronds. Largest is the mamaku (*C. medularis*) – its large fronds have black stipes or midribs and its trunk bears a pattern of large oval scars left by fallen fronds. This species is frequently seen on roadsides or forming a wonderful pattern with broadleaf trees on a hillside. The silver fern or ponga (*C. dealbata*), is the New Zealand national plant. The underside of its fronds and the central stipes are both silvery white. It is often found under the canopy, while mamaku tends to grow into or above it. Katote or soft tree fern (*C. smithii*) can be identified by its skirt of frond stipes hanging down around its trunk, while wheki-ponga (*D. fibrosa*) has a huge thick skirt of dead fronds. In contrast wheki (*D.squarrosa*) disposes of its fronds in a very casual way, giving the area in its immediate vicinity an untidy, littered appearance.

top Mamaku has oval frond scars. JF
right Silver fern is the national emblem. JF

FERN FRONDS

Fern fronds are most frequently composed of the central midrib or stipe, and the pinnae (from the Latin word for feather, which accurately describes their structure) that grow out from the midrib. The pinnae are usually paired leaflets. They may themselves be pinnate (divided), in which case the frond is bi-pinnate or twice-pinnate. Some fronds can be four times pinnate, and with some species the fronds only become three or four times pinnate with age.

Blechnum novae-zelandiae is a common roadside fern. JF

Once inside the forest you will find a bewildering array of ferns. There are over 165 species and many of them can only be identified by very close examination, particularly of the patterns made by the clusters (sori) of spore-producing cells on the underside of the fronds. Some are easy to identify, like the tiny floating fern *Azolla filiculoides*, which almost covers some lakes and ponds with its green and pink fronds; similarly distinctive are the large, drooping fronds of *Blechnum novae-zelandiae*, which are often seen on roadside banks. Others, such as the several species of filmy fern (*Hymenophyllum* spp.), with their graceful translucent fronds, need to be very closely examined if you want to identify them. Most ferns have pinnate or feathery fronds, but some have straight-edged or strap fronds, especially the genus *Grammitis*, of which *G. givenii* – often found on rocks or as an epiphyte on trees – is a common example. Also distinctive are some of the climbing ferns, especially kowaowao or hound's tongue (*Microsorum pustulatum*), whose long creeping rhizome is grey with black scales. The fronds start off as strap-shaped, but gradually become pinnate as the plant matures. Kowaowao tends to be a terrestrial creeper, but *Blechnum filiforme* is a common tree climber with fronds growing alternately from a central climbing rhizome.

Other distinctive species are the graceful umbrella fern (*Sticherus cunninghamii*) and the not dissimilar tangle fern (*Gleichenia dicarpa*), both of which prefer more open areas, with the latter forming a dense layered tangle of quite hard fronds.

Hen and chicken fern produces new plants directly from the fronds. JF

Commonly seem hanging from trees is the graceful drooping spleenwort (*Asplenium flaccidum*). Other species of the same genus have rather broader pinnae. Largest of the terrestrial ferns is the king fern (*Marattia salcinia*), whose fronds can be 4m long. At the other end of the scale, one of the smallest is the round-leaved kidney fern (*Trichomanes reniforme*), which often forms quite large patches in damp shady places. My favourite, though, is the hen and chicken fern (*Asplenium bulbiferum*), which reproduces not just via spores, but also by producing 'bulbils' or gametes, miniature ready-to-grow offspring, on its fronds.

FERN ALLIES

Three very different groups of plants are closely allied to the ferns. The Psilotopsida includes the rather broom-like *Psilotum nudum*, which has apparently leafless branches with clusters of yellow sporangia or spore capsules, and several species of fork fern. The Lycopsida has about a dozen species, including scrambling clubmoss (*Lycopodium volubile*) and alpine clubmoss (*L. fastigatum*), both of which look a bit like small shrubby mosses made of pipe cleaners. Last are the Equistopsida or horsetails such as the field horsetail (*Equisetum arvense*) – a dangerous invasive weed.

Scrambling clubmoss. TDR

Psilotum nudum. JF

BRYOPHYTES

Bryophytes are non-vascular plants. In other words they do not have a system of tubes for circulating liquids around their various parts. They do not produce flowers but reproduce by means of spores. There are three groups – mosses, liverworts and hornworts – all of which are represented in New Zealand.

Mosses (Bryophyta)

Given the relatively mild, often damp and shady conditions in New Zealand forests, it is not surprising that there are over 500 species of mosses here, found from the coast to near the snow line. Mosses have an intricate reproductive system, which is two-stage as in ferns, but the commonly seen visible plant is the gametophyte or sexually reproducing stage, and the sporophyte or spore-producing phase is a small plant that is parasitic on the parent.

Identifying mosses is definitely a hand lens or microscope job much of the time, but a few are readily identifiable for anyone – at least to genus level. The one you'll find easiest of all is the largest, *Dawsonia superba*, which produces individual spikes up to 50cm high, looking more like small pine seedlings than a moss. The wonderfully named *Dendroligotrichum dendroides* is similar, but smaller, darker green and branched. Known locally as 'old man's beard', *Weymouthia mollis* is commonly seen hanging in long strands from tree branches, producing an enchanting 'goblin wood' effect.

In wet upland areas there are several species of peat-forming sphagnum mosses, as well as round pincushions of the genus *Bryum* and the pipe-cleaner moss (*Ptichiomnion aciculare*), with its upright individual fronds. Two species found lower down are the soft mosses (*Dicranaloma* spp.), which often mix with other mosses and liverworts, and the milk moss (*Leucobryum candida*), with its milky green colouring.

'Old man's beard' *Weymouthia mollis* is common in very damp forest. JF

Liverworts (Marchantiophyta)

The common name for these simple plants derives from the old, unfounded belief that because many species had a liver-like shape, they would be good for treating liver ailments! This is a very ancient line of plants, going back some 400 million years. With over 500 species, 7% of the world total, New Zealand is liverwort-land. At first sight liverworts look very like some mosses and often grow mixed up with them. They come in two varieties: the leafy forms, which have leaves and are easily confused with some moss species, and the 'thalloids', which are flat sheets of cells. The latter are relatively easy to identify as liverworts – identifying them to any level beyond that becomes difficult. Closely related to liverworts are the hornworts, which resemble thalloid liverworts.

LICHENS

Lichens are widespread and common throughout New Zealand – there are probably over 2,000 types – but only 40% of them are endemic, compared with 84% of flowering plants. Lichens are not straightforward plants, but each is a symbiotic partnership between a fungus and a green or photosynthesising algae, or a cyanobacterium ('blue-green algae'), occasionally both. The fungus provides the algae or cyanobacterium with a 'home' and with minerals and water, which the algae uses to provide food, via photosynthesis, for itself and the fungus. The partnership is very stable and almost certainly extends the range of both partners. Lichens are very susceptible to aerial pollution, which is why they so enjoy New Zealand.

There are three types of lichen in New Zealand. Crustose lichens form a covering on the rock, tree, house or even road on which they grow. Many of these are almost circular and grow at a very steady rate – a tendency that has given rise to the science of 'lichenometry', or measuring the age of exposed surfaces such as lava flows by the age of the lichen growing on them. Foliose or leafy lichens are just that, and can be quite large and colourful. *Pseudocyphellaria homoeophylla* is bright green, while *Hypogymnia enteromorpha* is black and white. The third group are the fruticose or shrubby lichens, which have a bushy or shrubby appearance and they can often be found in the branches of trees. The coral or lace lichen (*Cladia repitora*) is a good and quite common example.

FUNGI

While often bracketed with the plants, fungi are not plants, but comprise a completely separate kingdom and are in fact more closely related to animals. There are thought to be around 1.5 million species worldwide, and probably some 22,000 species in New Zealand. The visible part of the fungus is just its reproductive part (fruiting body). The main body or mycelium lies within the soil, decaying leaves or wood, and consists of a network of root-like filaments called hyphae. The mycelium in some species can be very large indeed, covering several hectares.

The fungi you're most likely to see belong to the group called saprobics or decomposers, so called because they feed on decaying plant or animal tissues. Many produce noticeable, and sometimes edible, fruiting bodies. There are a number of different forms of fruiting body. Most common are the mushroom or gill fungi with their familiar umbrella shape. A commonly observed and easily identifiable species is the introduced scarlet flycap (*Amanita muscaria*), which is a gill fungus with a scarlet cap with white dots. You may recognise it from home as the fly agaric – its image is the standard representation for any magical or sinister toadstool. As with most mushroom types, they first emerge as a round ball with the umbrella shape developing as they grow. Bracket fungi stick out like a shelf from the trunk of a tree, first as a small white protrusion, then gradually growing into the shelf shape. Stinkhorns are often surprisingly phallic in shape and produce unpleasant smells, which attract flies to help in their propagation. Jelly fungi look just like that. Common jelly fungi include the hakeke or wood ears (*Auriculana* spp.). Puffballs are globular and release their spores through a hole at the top.

Do not eat any fungi unless you are certain they are edible: some are highly poisonous.

The scarlet flycap is introduced. JF

INTRODUCED PLANTS

The first settlers from Polynesia brought some plants with them, but they were all crop plants such as kumara, taro and gourds, and not at all invasive. With the arrival of European settlers, especially after 1840 when the agricultural industry started to develop, things changed and large numbers of new plants arrived, mainly from Europe but also from North America and Asia. Some species, such as grasses, crop plants and trees, were brought in deliberately, but the majority arrived as hitchhikers, mixed with seeds and soil. There are now well over 30,000 introduced plant species in New Zealand, over 2,000 of which have become naturalised. A significant number of these, such as gorse, broom, marram grass, various hawkweeds, willow, pines and tree lupins, have become serious pests, costing significant amounts of money to control and causing ecological change and damage to native species.

In urban and agricultural areas, the large majority of species that you see will be introduced. In Christchurch, known as the 'English city', it is quite hard to find native trees, though Wellington fares much better thanks to its rather hilly terrain. Not all introduced species are dangerous or damaging, but all have the potential to be, especially if climate change makes the climate more suitable for tropical species.

Native species arrived of their own accord and evolved here in balance with other species in the ecosystem. Any ecosystem can accommodate significant change if it occurs over a sufficient period of time. However, sudden changes such as the introduction of vigorous non-native species will unbalance the ecosystem and force some or most native species to extinction – only those that can adapt quickly will survive. The control elements – insects, disease, weather – that exist in the native ecosystems of aliens do not exist here. Left unchecked, these alien invaders will take over large areas of country to the virtual exclusion of all native species.

Broom is a colourful but destructive invasive species. JF

WHERE TO GO

The Bay of Islands seen from the top of Motuarohia, or Robertson Island. AD/TIPS

The biggest mistake many visitors make when planning to visit New Zealand is not allowing enough time. At first glance it is not a large country, and therefore you might think it ought to be fairly easy to see most of it, or at least the 'best bits', in a fairly short time – say two or three weeks. However, while the land area is only slightly larger than the UK's, at 269,000km², the country is over 1,600km long and is not only divided into three islands by the Cook and Foveaux straits, but for much of its length, from East Cape in the northeast to Fiordland in the southwest, it is divided by a mountain chain with only ten routes across it. There are no significant motorways outside of Auckland and most towns do not have bypasses, so road travel, while straightforward even on near-deserted roads, always takes a bit longer than you might expect. If it's at all possible, I would recommend allowing a minimum of one month if you want to see the best of both North and South Islands.

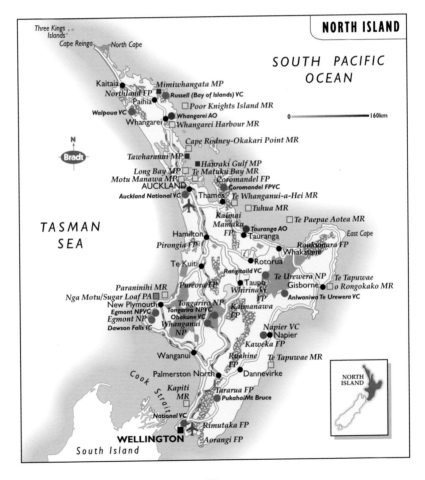

NATIONAL PARKS AND PROTECTED AREAS

National parks cover more than 30,000km² of New Zealand's finest landscapes and habitats, though high alpine and sub-alpine areas have disproportionately high representation. Hunting and fishing are allowed in most parks – the former activity is viewed as offering a degree of control over pest species such as possums, deer, goats and pigs.

Remember: you are not allowed to remove anything but rubbish or garbage from the parks. **Take only pictures and memories; leave only footprints.**

NORTH ISLAND NATIONAL PARKS

The more populated North Island has fewer national parks than South Island, but their accessibility makes them excellent places to observe native wildlife.

Te Urewera

This is the largest area of native forest in North Island, and a surprisingly remote and wild section of the country. The lakes of Waikaremoana and Waikareiti in the south of the park, along with the large areas of hills clad with native forest, are scenic highlights. Much of the forest is beech, especially in the north, with rimu-dominated podocarp in the south. All the native North Island bird species, apart from weka, are found here, with the scarce kokako in the north of the park. For the botanist there are over 650 species of flowering plant plus countless ferns, mosses and lichens. There are many hiking or tramping tracks; noteworthy is the three- or four-day Great Walk round Lake Waikaremoana, which has five overnight huts – you can book to stay at these or at one of a number of campsites. Lake Waikareiti was formed by a landslide that blocked the valley running down to Lake Waikaremoana.

Te Urawera is a strongly Maori area, home of the Ngai Tuhoe, 'The Children of the Mist', a fiercely independent *iwi*. The only road through it, SH38, is not sealed, so allow extra time if driving through. The highest mountain here is Manuoha, at 1,392m.

Tongariro

Sacred to the Maori, the three active volcanic peaks that make up this, New Zealand's first national park, were gifted to the nation in 1887 by Te Heuheu Tukino IV, paramount chief of the Ngati Tuwharetoa. For stark beauty, especially in winter, Tongariro is hard to beat, with eye-catching peaks in classically conical Mount Ngauruhoe and Mount Ruapehu – the latter, at 2,797m, the tallest volcano in New Zealand. The latter is still very active. Its last major eruption was in 1996, but its crater lake breaks out in lahars (mudslides) from time to time. Ngauruhoe may be familiar to you as Mount Doom in Peter Jackson's recent adaptation of *The Lord of the Rings*.

The park is an excellent area to observe alpine and sub-alpine habitats, with a number of good day-long tramping tracks, including the Tongariro Crossing, and the Tongariro Northern Circuit, which is a three/four-day tramp. There are 24 bookable overnight huts in the park. The forest is mainly beech. While native birds are around, they are relatively scarce due to the presence of introduced mammals.

Both native bats also occur in the park. Plant weed species are also a problem here with broom, heather and wilding pines being particular problems. Geologically the park is interesting for its many volcanic and glacial features.

Tongariro National Park is a double World Heritage Site, first for its natural values, and second for its cultural value. Initially, the World Heritage Committee declined to include it for its cultural value as there are no signs of cultural 'use', such as buildings or similar. However, following representations, the committee changed the rules and Tongariro became the first site recognised for its intangible cultural significance. There are three active ski-fields on Mount Ruapehu.

LORD OF THE RINGS

As aficionados will know, the recent *Lord of the Rings* trilogy was filmed in New Zealand, one of few countries that could offer the wild unspoilt landscape that was

such an integral part of the books. You can buy guides specifically devoted to exploring all of the various filming locations, and some general maps indicate the main locations. Sites are spread out, with quite a few in Tongariro and other national parks and a surprising number quite close to Wellington. There is another cluster around Queenstown and more around Lake Te Anau in Fiordland. While visiting all of these locations will not take you to the best wildlife sites, you'll see some wonderful, wild and unspoilt countryside, and add an interesting dimension to your travels.

Mount Ngauruhoe featured as Mount Doom in *Lord of the Rings*. C/TIPS

Whanganui

This is a lowland park centred around the Whanganui River to the west of Tongariro. Its highest point is Te Mapou at 746m. The park is dominated by podocarp broadleaf forest with rata, rimu, tawa and rewarewa prominent, and also has beech forest on the ridges. The river and its tributaries cut through soft mudstone, creating spectacular gorges and deep interlaced valleys. The river is an ideal habitat for the native blue duck or whio, and in the forest you can see kereru, tui, grey warbler, robin, tomtit and yellow-crowned parakeet. In the rivers you can also find native crayfish, eels, lampreys, galaxiids and the native freshwater flounder.

The park has important historical links for Maori and the river is very popular for river rafting and similar outdoor activities but the park itself, which is split into several separate areas alongside the river, has relatively few tramping tracks.

The whio or blue duck has benefited from an intensive conservation effort. TDR

Egmont

This almost perfectly circular national park is centred on the spectacular snow-capped volcanic cone of Mount Taranaki or Egmont. The park offers excellent opportunities to walk up from lush lowland or montane rainforest through sub-alpine bush, to alpine herbfields and fellfields – and even to the snow line. All the forest is podocarp broadleaf as beeches appear not to have re-colonised the area following the last ice age. There are some wonderful 'goblin forests' festooned with *Weymouthia* and other mosses, as well as a very good area of wetland: the Ahukawakawa Swamp – a must for botanists. There are a number of simple up-and-down hikes as well as a 'round the mountain' with good overnight huts. Birdlife includes kereru, tui, robin, tomtit, fantail, whitehead, yellow-crowned parakeet, rifleman, New Zealand falcon and morepork. There is also a wide variety of forest invertebrates.

NORTH ISLAND PROTECTED AREAS

There are 14 forest parks in North Island, all in upland areas apart from Northland Forest Park, which includes the finest remaining kauri trees as well as the museum on the history of kauri extraction. Coromandel, Kaimai Mamaku and Raukumara around the Bay of Plenty all offer a wide variety of native forest, including the southernmost kauri and the northernmost beech forests, while Whirinaki, adjacent to Te Urawera National Park, has some most impressive podocarp and tree fern combinations. The others all extend down the mountain ridge that forms the spine of North Island and, while much less visited, offer excellent forest walks and tramps. Pirongia in the Waikato is an island of uplands in a flat plain, while Pureora, west of Lake Taupo, forms the edge of the volcanic plateau. Both contain large areas of podocarp broadleaf forest and an excellent and varied wildlife. You can clearly see the effects of altitude on vegetation, with obvious changes as you ascend into the mountains. Pureora has a good 12m viewing tower to help you get closer to canopy birds – in other words, most forest birds.

There are a number of other conservation areas, including conservation parks, scenic reserves and so on, all of which provide an element of wilderness and offer wildlife-watching opportunities.

SOUTH ISLAND

0 ——————— 160km

TASMAN SEA

N
Bradt

Westhaven-Te Tai Tapu MR
Abel Tasman NP
Tonga Island MR
Horoirangi MR
Kahurangi NP
Nelson Regional VC
Westport
Nelson Lakes NPVC
Paparoa NPVC
Paparoa NP
Victoria FP
Greymouth
Hokitika
Arthur's Pass NP
Ross
Arthur's Pass NPVC
Craigieburn FP
Korowai/Torlesse Tussocklands Park
National VC
Westland/Tai Poutini NP
Westland/Tai Poutini NPVC
Aoraki/Mt Cook NP
Aoraki/Mt Cook NPVC
Haast VC
Mt Aspiring NP
Makarora VC
Ahuriri CP
Ruataniwha CP
Kaki/Black Stilt visitor hide
Glenorchy VC
Mt Aspiring NPVC
Fiordland Marine Reserves
Fiordland NP
Queenstown
Queenstown VC
Cromwell
Fiordland NPVC
Te Anau Wildlife Centre
Te Anau
Eyre Mountains/Taka Ra Haka CP
Te Papanui CP
Gore
Invercargill
Foveaux Strait
Catlins FP
Bluff
Rakiura NPVC
Oban
Rakiura NP
Ulva Island/Te Wharawhara MR
Stewart Island

Long Island-Kokomohua MR
North Island
Picton
Mt Richmond FP
Blenheim
Nelson Lakes NP
Hanmer FP
Kaikoura
Lake Sumner FP
Pegasus Bay
CHRISTCHURCH
Pohatu MR
Banks Peninsula Marine Area
Canterbury Bight
Timaru
Oamaru
Dunedin

Cook Strait

SOUTH PACIFIC OCEAN

SOUTH ISLAND

SOUTH ISLAND AND STEWART ISLAND NATIONAL PARKS
Abel Tasman
Situated at the northern end of South Island, Abel Tasman is the smallest of South Island's national parks and is noted for its coastline, especially the beaches, inlets and estuaries. The natural landscape has been considerably modified, so much of the bush is regenerating. There is both beech and podocarp-broadleaf forest and areas of geological interests. The many rocky outcrops – mainly granite, but some of limestone or marble – are linked to the karst limestone formation found inland on Takaka Hill. Birds here include kereru, tui, bellbird and fantail; watch out for the melanistic variety of the fantail here. The main tramping track here is around the coast, and there are many campsites as well as overnight huts. One of the most popular recreational pursuits here is kayaking, especially around the Tonga Island Marine Reserve. This is not a wildlife hotspot but is a very pleasant and relaxing area.

Tree ferns and podocarps in a wet west coast forest. TDR

Kahurangi

In contrast, Kahurangi, at over 4,500km², is one of the largest parks and covers much of northwestern South Island. It contains a wide variety of habitats and wildlife and has excellent tramping tracks, most notably the Heaphy, which, at 82km, is the longest of the 'Great Walks'. This trail takes you from Golden Bay across to the west coast. Much of the park is in the alpine and sub-alpine zone, with a wonderful flora. It is also the last major refuge of the huge *Powelliphanta* snails and one of their favourite prey items, the native earthworm which can be up to a metre long. The central and western part of the park is not easily accessed, as there are few trails. Birds here include great spotted kiwi, tui, bellbird, kereru, morepork, New Zealand falcon, blue duck and rifleman. Long-tailed bats are also here, but like so much native wildlife, they are nocturnal and so you'll need perseverance, patience and luck to spot them.

Paparoa

This small park on the west coast is centred on the remarkable pancake rocks at Punakaiki. These strange, evenly layered and unevenly weathered limestone formations are a major attraction. Inland the vegetation is a lush temperate rainforest with good examples of podocarp-broadleaf forest, and nikau palms in the lower areas. Higher inland the forest turns to beech. There are kiwis here, along

with the usual forest birds – tui, bellbird and kereru. South of the Punakaiki River is the world's only breeding site of the Westland petrel, a large dark petrel that flies inland at dusk and returns to sea before dawn.

Karst limestone at Takaka Hill. JF

Nelson Lakes

This park covers some 1,020km² at the northern end of the Southern Alps. It is a land of forested mountains and deep glacial valleys. Lakes Rotoiti and Rotoroa – not to be confused with Rotorua and Rotoiti on North Island – fill two of these spectacular valleys. The Buller River flows out of Rotoiti and is supplemented by the Gowan flowing out of Rotoroa; there is something special about seeing the birth of a river. The highest peak is Mount Franklin at 2,340m. The park has a number of tramping tracks and overnight huts; the best-known trail is the Travers Sabine Track, which connects the two lakes.

The forest is largely beech; black beech high up and red and silver beech closer to the lakes. Beech woods are generally not quite as rich in wildlife as podocarp-broadleaf as there is much less undergrowth and fewer tree species, but it is an excellent place to see tomtits, robins and the rifleman, the last with its almost inaudibly high-pitched call. Kaka, the native forest parrot, is also around and great spotted kiwis were reintroduced here in 2004. With beech forest the tree line can be very abrupt: all of a sudden you are out of the forest and onto alpine herbfields and fellfields. In late spring and summer these are thick with alpine flowers: large alpine daisies, amazing boulder-like vegetable sheep, mat plants, prostrate shrubs, sundews, buttercups... the variety is huge. Keep an eye open here for alpine lizards and *Powelliphanta*, the giant carnivorous land snails, as well as alpine grasshoppers, cicadas and dragonflies.

The Rotoiti Nature Recovery Project at the St Arnaud end of Lake Rotoiti is well worth a visit. It is an area of 'honeydew beech forest' that has been made into a 'mainland island' by intensive predator and wasp controls. Listen out for bellbirds and tuis here.

The Waimakiriri River, Arthur's Pass. JF

Arthur's Pass

In the middle of South Island, this mountainous park straddles the divide and has beech forest to the east contrasting with luxuriant podocarp-broadleaf rainforest to the west. Easily accessible by both road and rail, there is a lot to observe here, from the masses of wild flowers along high alpine walks up side valleys, to wrybills on the braided rivers. One bird you need to watch out for is the kea, the alpine parrot, which is adept at damaging cars and backpacks. To the east there are areas of tussock grassland, with lakes on which you may spot Australasian crested grebes, black-billed gulls and black-fronted terns. The high alpine area is home to one of New Zealand's smallest birds, the rock wren. Here too you can see the northern rata in all its glory from December through February.

There are many walks in the park, varying from an hour or so to a good day's tramp. You can also take longer, more arduous overnight tramps, using some of the many huts. All of the longer walks take you up above the tree line to the alpine areas.

Aoraki Mount Cook

Aoraki is the Maori name for Mount Cook. The peak and its surrounds are sacred to the Ngai Tahu, who are this region's *tangata whenua* or 'people of the land'. Aoraki Mount Cook and Westland National Park are contiguous, Aoraki Mount Cook being to the east of the divide and Westland to the west. Aoraki Mount Cook is a high alpine and mountainous park including Aoraki Mount Cook, at 3,754m the highest peak in New Zealand. The park also features the two longest glaciers in New Zealand: the Tasman and Hooker. There is virtually no forest, but wonderful alpine uplands with a wide range of plants, including the metre-high Mount Cook lily, which is actually a white buttercup, and the rather fearsomely spined spaniards. Alpine skinks and geckos have been found in the park, so keep an eye open, and there are the usual alpine invertebrates around. The braided riverbed of the Tasman is a breeding area for the critically endangered black stilt. There are several tramping trails, some of which require a fair degree of fitness, and also many more mountainous hikes and climbs, with the usual excellent huts.

Mount Sefton towers 3,151m high in the snow-capped Southern Alps. TDR

Fox Glacier is one of two that flow down from Mount Cook and come within 20km of the coast. TDR

Westland – Tai Poutini

The Westland park covers the rainforest on the west of the divide and runs down to the coast. It includes the two most accessible glaciers in New Zealand, the Fox and Franz Joseph. Their snouts, both of which are currently receding, are accessible by easy trails. The vegetation varies from high alpine meadows and fellfields, through beech forest to lush podocarp-broadleaf rainforest and on to the coastal wetlands and lagoons. This results in a wide variety of plant and animal species, though access is not easy due largely to the steep nature of the terrain and the rainfall, which can be as much as 12m a year high up (reducing to

Fox Glacier snout. JF

Westland National Park offers challenging terrain to hikers. TDR

a mere 5m on the coast). Lake Mapourika is a good place to see the Australasian crested grebe and at nearby Okarito Lagoon there are wading birds, including royal spoonbill and white heron. Around Okarito on the coast you can also see the endangered Okarito brown kiwi.

The Alpine Fault runs through the park and is responsible for the abrupt and dramatic change from steep mountainside to flat lowland. If you are feeling extravagant, a flight over the glaciers and snowfields of the area is an unforgettable experience and a great lesson in glaciology.

Westland National Park is are part of the Te Wahipounamu South West New Zealand World Heritage area, which also includes the Mount Aspiring and Fiordland National Parks.

Mount Aspiring

Further south and very mountainous, this park has the 3,030m Mount Aspiring as its highest point. It is very much a walker's park and includes one end of the famous Routeburn Track, a tourist tramp used as long ago as 1880. The forest here is beech and there are large areas of alpine herbfield and fellfield, resulting in a wide variety of species, including rock wren, kea, alpine geckos and skinks, kereru, yellowhead, rifleman, morepork and the two native bats.

Fiordland

By far the largest of New Zealand's national parks, Fiordland is a huge area of remote mountains and valleys, rivers and lakes, including the two largest, Te Anua and Manapouri. Access to much of the park is not easy due to the terrain but there are some great hikes, including the Routeburn and Milford tracks. Wildlife here originally included the flightless takahe and kakapo. The wild populations of both have been removed and are now being captive-reared in safety, mainly on island nature reserves. Vegetation varies from alpine to coastal rainforest, with rainfall up to 12m a year, and so there is a wide variety of plants, over 700 species, as well as birds and invertebrates including, annoyingly, the sandfly or namu.

The New Zealand dotterel is one of the most endangered species in New Zealand. JF

Rakiura

Rakiura covers 85% of Stewart Island. Much of it is podocarp-broadleaf forest; there are no beeches here. The peaks of Mount Anglem in the north and Mount Allen in the south have alpine and sub-alpine vegetation, while in the central area there are extensive wetlands, and in the west large areas of sand dunes, rising to 150m, inland from Mason Bay. Ecologically, Stewart Island is a world of its own, and while white-tailed deer and other pest species abound, an eradication programme is starting in 2008 to clear the whole island. At 1,700km², Stewart Island will be by far the largest island ever subjected to such a project in New Zealand. There are several hiking tracks, including a fairly strenuous round-the-island track, and a rather easier one across to Mason Bay. Wildlife includes Stewart Island brown kiwi, over at Mason Bay, and on Ulva Island you may see weka, kea, tui, brown creeper, kereru and yellow-crowned parakeet. On the coast you can find the Stewart Island shag as well as a number of waders and the New Zealand pipit.

SOUTH ISLAND PROTECTED AREAS

South Island has seven forest parks and four conservation parks. Among these are Craigieburn and Lake Sumner, which offer wonderful upland and alpine experiences, and the Catlins on the southeast coast has some of the least affected rainforest in the country and is additionally right next to a wild and fascinating coastal area. As in the North Island there are too many protected areas to mention all of them, but they are all worth a visit and enhance the overall wildlife and wilderness experience.

PHOTOGRAPHY

New Zealand offers some wonderful opportunities for both scenic and wildlife photography, so make sure you have enough storage capacity in the form of memory cards, or bring a good way of downloading your images. One point to be aware of is that the air is very clear and the light is very bright. This makes it easy to overexpose and can make photographs very contrasty; sometimes bright but cloudy days are the best – especially in the forest.

ACTIVITIES

With such a variety of environments and well-developed tourist infrastructure, you are spoilt for choice for things to do and see in New Zealand's great outdoors.

SPORTING ACTIVITIES

New Zealand is a very outdoor-oriented country; almost everyone seems to get involved in one outdoor activity or another, sometimes several. It is a young and in some respects a frontier society, which is reflected in the passion for hunting and fishing. With 32 introduced mammal species, there are plenty of hunting targets – deer, goats, chamois and pigs for starters, all of which are serious pest animals. Hunting with a permit is allowed in most national parks and other protected areas, and is enjoyed by many, both those who live in the country and the cities.

Fishing is probably more popular. New Zealand has the highest per capita boat ownership in the world, with many of those boats being used primarily for fishing, both in inland lakes and around the coast. This is also linked in with the Maori communities' historic reliance on fish and shellfish, which they still retain. Until recently there had been a plentiful supply of fish, but with the increasingly advanced systems used by amateurs, fishing now seems to be having an impact on stocks and catch sizes. The use of mini long lines and lines launched from the beach is common; how about kite fishing where you can fish up to 2km offshore from the beach! Then there is trout fishing in the rivers, especially in South Island, and the national excitement with the onset of the whitebait season in the spring. Fishing crosses all barriers and is a good indicator of the level society that New Zealand aspires to be.

Mountain biking is an increasingly popular sport, with many trails specifically designed for it. Biking is encouraged in many protected areas, though not in national parks where tramping is still king. It is easy to hire bikes in most parts of New Zealand and you can join organised groups as well.

Watersports such as surfing, windsurfing, kite surfing, kayaking, white-water rafting, sledging and paragliding are all popular – you name it, you can do it in New Zealand, and there are plenty of places where you can do it as a tourist. There are, of course, more extreme sports around, such as sky-diving and bungee-jumping off the sky-tower in Auckland; if it's do-able, then it can and will be done here.

Skiing and snowboarding are popular, with opportunities in Tongariro National Park on the slopes of Ruapehu, and further south around Queenstown – which is the main winter sports centre for the country. The season is generally from late June through October, though generally longer in the south than in the north.

Feral pigs are widespread and provoke a conflict between conservationists who want to eradicate them and hunters who want to keep them. JF

Kayaking is another very popular recreational activity – and at times a very practical one and great for wildlife-watching. You can hire kayaks almost anywhere that they can be used: on rivers, lakes or the sea. They can take you to places that are otherwise inaccessible on foot or by car. You can generally hire single or double kayaks, and in some places Canadian canoes are also available.

TRAMPING

Tramping (hiking) is one of the most popular outdoor activities. Something like 43% of the land area is either native forest or alpine herbfields and fellfields, which allows for a rich variety of walks and tramping trails – from ten minutes to ten days. Tramping tracks are mainly constructed and maintained by the Department of Conservation, which also constructs and maintains the many excellent overnight huts that make long-distance tramping a reasonable option. So popular are some of the tracks, such as the Milford and Routeburn, that you have to book months in advance to reserve a bunk in a hut, and on the Milford Track numbers are strictly limited. There are many other tracks that are little used, especially midweek and out of the peak season (which runs from Christmas to the end of January). If you want to you can easily get away from it all, either in deep tracts of native bush in the Uraweras or high up on the alpine ridges of the Southern Alps.

If you plan to do anything other than day tramps, then it pays to plan well in advance, book huts if necessary and check out the likely weather conditions for that area at that time of year. Weather in New Zealand is notoriously fickle and, especially in the mountains, can change very rapidly. Always wear hiking boots and carry warm and waterproof clothing, let someone know where you are going and when you expect to be back. Take nothing for granted: the wilderness can be very unforgiving.

There are nine trips that are classified by DOC as 'Great Walks'. If you do them all, you will experience a lot of New Zealand's wild and wonderful scenery and wildlife.

Lake Waikaremoana Track A 46km three- or four-day hike around Lake Waikaremoana in the Te Urawera National Park.

Tongariro Northern Circuit A three- or four-day hike around the volcanoes of the Tongariro National Park.

Whanganui Journey Not a walk, but a three- to five-day river trip in kayaks thorough the Whanganui National Park.

Abel Tasman Coastal Track A 51km, three- to five-day hike around the coast of the Abel Tasman National Park.

Heaphy Track An 82km, four- to six-day hike across the Kahurangi National Park from Golden Bay to the west coast.

Routeburn Track A 32km, two- or three-day hike through the Mount Aspiring and Fiordland national parks.

Milford Track A 53km four-day hike through Fiordland National Park. Booking essential in peak periods.

Kepler Track A 60km three- or four-day hike in Fiordland National Park.

Rakiura Track – Round the Island Track A 36km three-day hike, extendable via the Round the Island Track to six or seven days, through the Rakiura National Park on Stewart Island.

Full details of all walks are available on the Department of Conservation website: www.doc.govt.nz.

The alpine areas of New Zealand offer true wilderness and solitude. NF

MOUNTAINEERING

One of New Zealand's most famous favourite sons was Sir Edmund Hillary, affectionately known as 'Sir Ed', the first man up Everest. Sir Ed honed his mountaineering skills in the Southern Alps, and today New Zealand offers many opportunities for the enthusiastic mountaineer. There are a number of local climbing clubs, and one national organisation, the New Zealand Alpine Club. As with all adventure sports, be sure to discuss your plans with local people and ensure that they are aware where you are going and when you expect to return. Take a mobile phone.

WILDLIFE HOTSPOTS

Although New Zealand's national parks and Great Walks will allow you to see a good variety of native wildlife, you will probably also want to visit at least some of the areas where the scarcest of the native species can be found, thanks to the absence of alien plants and animals.

MAINLAND ISLANDS

New Zealand has pioneered the concept of creating 'inland islands' – areas where all or most pest species have been eradicated to enable the natives to flourish. These fall into two categories: the fenced and the unfenced. Fencing the area off is clearly the ideal, as a physical barrier makes it very hard for pests to re-colonise. But the cost of doing this is enormous, so for many areas, especially larger ones like the DOC Mainland Islands, going fenceless is the only realistic option.

Fenced islands

Karori Sanctuary, probably the best-known inland sanctuary, is only five minutes from the centre of Wellington and is easily accessible by public transport. It is a 2.52km^2 reserve centred on the Karori Valley, which was partially flooded in 1871 to provide Wellington's water supply. It is now surrounded by an 8.6km predator-proof fence and all introduced predators have been eradicated. Among a variety of indigenous species now found there are little spotted kiwi, morepork, tui, bellbird, stitchbird and tuatara. There are also some great weta hotels, glow-worms and an excellent new visitor and education centre. This sanctuary has become a centre for avian biodiversity for all of Wellington.

Tawharanui Open Sanctuary is a fenced-off peninsula north of Auckland, near Warkworth, which is open to the public. The major pest eradication was done in 2004, but the process continues in an effort to eradicate rabbits, mice and hedgehogs. The sanctuary offers good examples of lowland and coastal bush, including kauri, rimu, tawa and puriri, as well as some fine pohutakawa on the cliffs. The coastal wetlands and dunelands offer a variety of walks and cycle tracks. Birds here include bellbirds and fantails in the bush, Australasian bittern, spotless crake, brown teal and fernbird in the wetlands, and New Zealand dotterel, reef heron and oystercatchers on the shore.

The grey duck has a striking head pattern, but often hybridises with introduced mallards. TDR

Maungatautari Ecological Island on North Island has the longest pest-proof fence of all. It stretches for 47km, around Maungatautari, an isolated 800m volcanic cone in the Waikato Plain south of Hamilton. Initial eradication started in two enclosures in 2004, with the process extended to the whole reserve in 2006 and 2007, while the fence itself was completed in August 2007. Kakas, brown kiwis and takahes have been released. The kiwis have already produced young and further introductions will be made as the forest recovers. Native birds there already include grey duck, Australasian bittern, shining cuckoo, morepork, tui, bellbird and kereru, some 25 species in all. There is also an excellent 18m viewing tower enabling you to see into and above the canopy.

Bushy Park is an area of lowland native rainforest near Wanganui on North Island with a 4.6km pest-excluding fence that was completed in 2005. Several species, including North Island brown kiwi and saddleback, have been reintroduced. There are various walks through the forest, whose trees include northern rata, pukatea, kahikatea, miro and matai. There is a wetland area and invertebrates are common, including cicadas, huhu beetles and the wonderful giraffe weevil with its immensely long snout.

Orokonui Eco-sanctuary is just north of Dunedin on South Island and is a 3km^2 sanctuary with a 10km pest fence around it. It includes regenerating native lowland forest as well as wetlands and open water, and boasts at least 11 species of native freshwater fish. Pest eradication was finalised in 2008. Birds here include tomtit, rifleman, brown creeper, fantail, bellbird and grey warbler, and as the project develops kiwis and other species will be introduced.

There are many other smaller fenced reserves, including Riccarton Bush in Christchurch and Young Nick's Head in Hawkes Bay. The object at the latter has been to protect a colony of grey-faced petrels, but it has also benefited geckos, skink and weta. Many of these smaller fenced reserves are private initiatives.

Unfenced islands

Unfenced mainland 'islands' are created by an intensive pest-eradication campaign, and their pest-free status is maintained by a long-term extensive monitoring programme. A number of these are particularly noteworthy and worth visiting.

Tree ferns and broadleaf/podocarp forest in the Waitakere Ranges. TDR

Ark in the Park is a large native-species recovery project in the Waitakere Ranges to the west of Auckland. It is a joint venture between Auckland Regional Council and Forest & Bird. Pest control on the first 2.5km² was started in 2003, extended to 10km² in 2005 and then to 20km² in 2008. The park is all native forest, including kauri and other large podocarps. Reintroduced birds include robin, whitehead and stitchbird, with plans afoot for kokako, bellbird, parakeet and kaka, along with lizards, invertebrates, such as giant weta, and plants, such as mistletoe. There are a good variety of day walks here.

Hinewai is a private reserve on the Banks Peninsula near Christchurch on South Island, run by the Maurice White Native Forest Trust. This reserve has grown from an initial 1.09km² to 12.9km². It runs from a height of over 600m with sub-alpine vegetation to near sea level, with plans to extend to the coast in the future. The focus here is mainly on restoring the native vegetation by controlling possums and eliminating invasive plants, but birds are returning, with fantail, tui and morepork seen regularly.

Otanewainuku Kiwi Trust, in the Bay of Plenty, manages 1,200ha of virgin bush with an intensive pest-control regime and a predator-proof crèche area for kiwi chicks. This is some of the best lowland broadleaf/podocarp forest in North Island and also has kereru, tui, bellbird, grey warbler, tomtit, kokako, fantail, North Island robin, long-tailed bats, geckos and skinks.

Not to be confused with Lake Rotoiti near Rotorua in Bay of Plenty, the **Rotoiti Nature Recovery Project** focuses on an area of honeydew beech forest on the shores of Lake Rotoiti in the Nelson Lakes National Park. Pest eradication covers not just the usual mammalian culprits of possum, deer, stoats and rats, but also introduced wasps that consume the honeydew produced by the honeydew scale insect *Ultracoeolstoma*. The project covers over 50km^2 and ensures that bellbirds abound as well as brown kiwis, kakas and other forest species.

DOC runs a programme of six Mainland Islands, all unfenced. In North Island these include Trounson Kauri Park in Northland; the Northern Te Urawera Ecological Restoration Project, which includes almost all native North Island bird species; Paengaroa, a small 1.17km^2 reserve near Taihape, noted for having over 30 species of divaricating shrub; and Boundary Stream near Napier, with kokako, kiwi, lizards and Powelliphanta snails. Similar projects on South Island include the Rotoiti Lake project mentioned above and the largest of them, the Hurunui Mainland Island in North Canterbury, covering more that 120km^2. More than 30 native bird species have been recorded at Hurunui, including kaka, New Zealand falcon, shining cuckoo, kea, great spotted kiwi and yellow-crowned parakeet.

ISLAND SANCTUARIES AND MARINE RESERVES

New Zealand is fortunate to have a large number of islands around its coasts, varying from islets of well under a hectare to Great Barrier Island, which covers an area of 285km^2 and reaches a height of 621m. With the destruction of the native forest and the eradication of many native bird and invertebrate species on much of the three main islands, these islands have become precious refuges for wildlife and have since been used as part of an extensive and sophisticated recovery programme. A number of these offshore nature reserves, such as Codfish and Little Barrier Island, are off-limits without a special permit. However, three are readily accessible – though bookings are essential, especially in the peak season.

The small, 2.2km^2 **Tiritiri Matangi Island** in the Hauraki Gulf is one of the premier wildlife locations in New Zealand. Originally farmed, the last livestock were removed in 1971. This was followed by a huge forest restoration when 280,000 trees were planted by volunteers. Native bird species, such as North Island brown kiwi, stitchbird, saddleback, bellbird, takahe and kokako, were subsequently reintroduced. While you can make a day trip to the island, an overnight stay is better to ensure you don't miss the amazing dawn chorus, and the chance to see kiwi, which are nocturnal. This is without doubt the best place in New Zealand to see many native forest birds.

Pohutakawa in full bloom on Tiritiri Matangi Island. TDR

Kapiti Island, just north of Wellington on the west coast, is another sheep farm turned nature reserve. A long, narrow 20km² island with a near-vertical western cliff face, it is now pest-free and is accessible on a daily basis. Here again an overnight stay is highly recommended as an opportunity to see the little spotted kiwi. The island vegetation is regenerating strongly and among the bird species you can see and hear are robin, bellbird, tui, stitchbird, red-crowned parakeet and, in summer, long-tailed cuckoo. There are wading birds in the lagoon at the northern end of the island including royal spoonbill and variable oystercatcher, while breeding seabirds include white-fronted terns and black-backed gulls.

Matui or **Somes Island** is the smallest of the three but, as it is situated in the middle of Wellington Harbour, it is also the most accessible and ideally suited for a day trip. Pests were eradicated in 1980 and it is now an excellent place to see the kakariki or red-crowned parakeet, North Island robin, fantail and a variety of seabirds, including the little blue penguin. A recent first was the successful hatching of a tuatara, and there are seven species of gecko and skink on the island as well as over 500 species of invertebrate, including at least two species of weta. Major habitat restoration has replaced introduced plant species with natives, thus encouraging other native species to become established.

MARINE RESERVES

With over 15,000km of coastline, a great many islands and a marine fauna under pressure from commercial, sport and local fishing, New Zealand has wisely established a number of marine reserves that help to preserve as much as possible of the marine life of the archipelago. It has also developed a fairly comprehensive set of regulations for all fishers to help protect stocks. So successful have the reserves been that it is not uncommon to see fishers anchored just outside the reserve, knowing that there are more fish in the reserve than outside it, and that they will sometimes be tempted to wander out of their safe haven.

Given the length of coastline and number of islands, the total of 12 reserves in North Island and 16 in South Island, many of those in Fiordland, suggests that there is potential for increasing the number of reserves, especially in the north of North Island where pressure on stocks is greatest and there are large number of amateur and local fishers.

OTHER WILDLIFE LOCATIONS

There are many other great places to see birds and other wildlife in New Zealand outside the national parks, island reserves and inland islands. Here are some of them.

North Island

Great Barrier Island is the largest island in the Hauraki Gulf and is 60% administered by DOC. It has a number of good locations for brown teal, black petrel, banded rail, grey warbler, little blue penguin and other seabirds around the coast.

The **Miranda Shorebird Centre** in the Firth of Thames is *the* place for waders, with 43 species recorded here and a total list of over 130 species. There are 85km² of mudflats so a high-tide visit is essential. This site also has a chenier beach (made up almost entirely of mollusc shells), one of only three in the southern hemisphere.

The **Mount Bruce National Wildlife Centre** is located 30km north of Masterton on SH2. It is a breeding centre for endangered species, including kaka, kokako, brown kiwi, stitchbird and yellow-crowned parakeet. There are also walks through ancient podocarp forest and good birdwatching opportunities. It also has the most easily viewed tuataras.

Otari Wilton Bush is a wonderful reserve, right on the edge of Wellington and accessible by public transport. It has 1km² of native forest and 5ha of botanic garden devoted entirely to native species. A survey, the Bioblitz, in 2007 counted over 1,300 species of plants, fungi, invertebrates and birds, including a new species of cave weta and a new fungus.

South Island

Situated midway between Picton and Christchurch, **Kaikoura** is a haven for ocean wildlife. Deep underwater canyons just offshore bring a huge variety of marine life to Kaikoura, including whales, dolphins, several species of albatross and numerous smaller petrels and shearwaters, skuas, gulls and terns. You can book boat trips throughout the year. Large flocks of Hutton's shearwaters can be seen close to the coast, especially north of Kaikoura.

There is a captive breeding programme at **Twizel** for the black stilt. You can watch these endangered birds from the Black Stilt Visitor Hide.

A wildlife centre next to the **Fiordland Visitor Centre**, Te Anau, has takahe, weka, yellow-crowned parakeet, tui, kea and kaka.

At the tip of the Otago Peninsula near Dunedin, **Taiaroa Head** is the only mainland albatross colony in the world. There are around 30 pairs of northern royal albatross here, as well as an excellent visitor and viewing centre. You can see other species too, such as little blue and yellow-eyed penguins, Stewart Island and spotted shags, and various waders and waterfowl. Keep an eye open for fur seals on the rocky shoreline.

LOOK AROUND YOU
Whenever you are out walking, hiking or tramping, take your time to look around you, try not just to put your head down and aim for the waterfall or viewpoint as fast as possible. Notice the details – the tiny ground-hugging shrubs and plants, the tangle of supplejack or divaricating shrubs. Look for trees' juvenile stages and observe the amazing variety of glossy green leaves; you'll be amazed by how many variations of the colour green are on show. Ferns are one of the wonders of the bush, as are the mosses, liverworts and lichens. Enjoy the small and unusual as well as the big and spectacular. Take time, listen to the birdsong, absorb and appreciate.

Many of the native forest birds prefer to be up in the canopy rather than on the ground, so a good pair of binoculars will enhance your experience. Also if you are interested in seabirds, binoculars are essential for identifying or getting a good look. You should aim for a waterproof pair with 8 or 10 times magnification.

TOP BIRDWATCHING LOCATIONS
If the focus of your trip is birdwatching, the sites listed below are all excellent and would form the basis of a great birdwatching itinerary. One of the high points of New Zealand birdwatching is seeing (and identifying) the masses of waders that visit muddy shorelines. Wader-watching is nearly always best around high tide, and of course most of the migrants are only here during the southern summer from October through to March or April. Most estuaries offer birdwatching opportunities year-round, but the larger ones are difficult to access so you may be better off looking at some of the smaller ones.

Sites already mentioned: North Island
All four national parks
Trounson Kauri Park
Tiritiri Matangi Island
Tawharanui Open Sanctuary
Ark in the Park – Auckland

Maungatautari Ecological Island
Te Urawera, Tongariro and Egmont national parks
Otanewainuku (Te Puke, Bay of Plenty)
Pureora and Pirongia forest parks
Waitomo Caves – Te Kuiti
Young Nick's Head – Hawkes Bay
Bushy Park – Wanganui
Karori Sanctuary – Wellington
Kapiti Island

Sites already mentioned: South Island and Stewart Island
All ten national parks
Lake Rotoiti Nature Recovery Project
Hurunui Mainland Island
Hinewai
Orokonui

Other good birdwatching locations
Northland
- Karikari Peninsula
- Whangarei Harbour, including Ruakaka Harbour and Bream Head
- Kaipara Harbour – Manukapua Island and other sites
- Waipu Estuary
Auckland
- Muriwai gannet colony
Waikato and Coromandel
- Miranda Shore Bird Centre
- Whangamarino Wetlands – Off SH1 south of Mercer
Bay of Plenty
- Tauranga, Maketu and Ohiwa harbours
East coast
- Cape Kidnappers gannet colony
- Ocean Beach Wildlife Preserve – includes Cape Kidnappers
- Hawkes Bay wetlands – Lake Tutira and Lake Waikopiro
Wanganui
- Manawatu Estuary
Wellington
- Owhiro Bay to Palmer Head – little blue penguins and rock pools
- Somes Island in Wellington Harbour
Nelson and Marlborough
- Queen Charlotte Sound
- French Pass
Tasman and Nelson
- Farewell Spit – gannet colony and a variety of shorebirds

Canterbury and Otago
- Christchurch – Bromley Oxidation Ponds and Avon-Heathcote Estuary
- Lake Ellesmere – between Christchurch and Akaroa
- Inland lakes and braided rivers
- Mackenzie Basin and Ahuriri River

Westland
- Okarito Lagoon
- Waitangiroto Nature Reserve – white heron sanctuary

Southland and Stewart Island
- Oamaru penguin colonies
- Nugget Point
- Catlins Lake and Estuary
- Fortrose Lagoon
- Awarua Bay
- New River Estuary

GETTING OFFSHORE

New Zealand has recorded an impressive 100 species of seabird. It is well worth trying to get offshore to enjoy close encounters with them, and there are, especially in North Island, many opportunities to do this. You also stand a good chance of seeing seals, sea lions, whales and dolphins. The ferry crossings of Cook Straight and Foveaux Straight can yield albatrosses and other offshore birds. Good spots include:
- Bay of Islands
- Hauraki Gulf
- Bay of Plenty – Tauranga and Whakatane for White Island
- Wellington Harbour – for Somes Island
- Kaikoura
- Milford Sound

PLANNING AND TRAVEL

When planning your trip, allow plenty of time and do not be too ambitious. It is not realistic to allow less than two weeks for each island, and you could easily allow a month each and still have left a lot out. While roads are good, and often have little traffic, they are not motorways and most journeys take longer than trips of equivalent mileages would back home. There are places of interest throughout the country, from the kauri forests in Northland to the kiwis, keas and wekas on Stewart Island in the far south. If you do not have at least a month, try not to cover the whole country, concentrate on a smaller area and come back for a second visit later!

CAMPER VANS

Due to the limitations of New Zealand's public transport network, you'll probably want to get around by road. Buses are an option if you have time and hitchhiking is still quite acceptable, though the lack of traffic in some areas, such as the west coast, can mean that long waits are to be expected. So for most people at least some travel will involve a car – or the ever-popular camper van. Land of birds, land of trees, land of lichens, land of beetles… and New Zealand is most certainly also a land of camper vans. This is a very popular mode of travel, with tourists using everything from the enormous 'house bus' to the very basic small converted van. There are regulations regarding off-road camping with vans; check that your van is fitted with the necessary facilities.

CAMPING AND CAMPSITES

Most commercial campsites offer sites for tents, and camping in the wild is permitted in many areas. DOC offer generally good facilities in the national parks and other protected areas; you can easily obtain a map from them showing all their campsites.

Facilities for camping and campers are many, varied and generally very good, ranging from quite luxurious campsites with top-class facilities, to fairly basic DOC sites in wilder areas. Also available at many campsites are chalets and cooking facilities, so travelling by car and using these can be an economic compromise.

PUBLIC TRANSPORT

There are only three long-distance passenger train lines in New Zealand, largely due to the mountainous nature of the country. Those three – Auckland to Wellington, Picton to Christchurch and Christchurch to Greymouth – offer passengers a spectacular and comfortable way of travelling and seeing parts of the country not easily visited by road or foot. Services are more frequent from November through April, and booking is essential. The Auckland to Wellington run takes you over the volcanic plateau and past the three magnificent volcanoes of the Tongariro National Park, and includes the very unusual Raurimu spiral where the line passes over itself to gain height. Picton to Christchurch follows the coast for much of the way and enables you to stop off at Kaikoura for seabird- and whale-watching, while the Tranz-Alpine from Christchurch to Greymouth goes through Arthur's Pass and provides a very special view of the alpine wonderland and heavily wooded western escarpment.

Getting around by bus is entirely possible, and is probably the least expensive way to travel. Certainly there are good and regular services between all the major towns and cities. Some of the major wildlife attractions, such as Kaikoura and Waitomo Caves, can be reached by bus, but smaller, more specialised places are harder to get to.

FURTHER INFORMATION

BOOKS
There are many books that will help you to understand and appreciate the biodiversity of New Zealand, as well as guides to specific groups, such as birds, plants or insects. The list below covers most of the good ones.

FIELD GUIDES
These are all books that you can put in your pocket or day pack when going for a walk.

General
Nature Guide to New Zealand Forest, John Dawson and Rob Lucas, Godwit, 2000.
From Weta to Kauri, Janet Hunt and Rob Lucas, Random House New Zealand, 2004.
The Reed Field Guide to Alpine Flora and Fauna, Brian Parkinson,
Raupo Publishing Ltd, 2001.
The Natural History of New Zealand, Julian Fitter, David Bateman Ltd /
Christopher Helm, 2009.

Birds
Hand Guide to the Birds of New Zealand, Barrie Heather, Hugh Robertson and Derek Onley, Penguin Books, 1999.
Birds of New Zealand: A Photographic Guide, Geoff Moon, New Holland, 2002.
Which New Zealand Bird?, Andrew Crowe, Penguin Books, 2001.
Albatross: Their World, their Ways, Tui De Roy, Mark Jones and Julian Fitter,
Christopher Helm, 2008.

Plants
Stewart Island Plants, Hugh D Wilson, Field Guide Publications, 1982.
Wild Plants of Mount Cook National Park, Hugh D Wilson, Field Guide Publications, 1978.
Which Native Fern?, Andrew Crowe, Penguin Books, 2001.
Field Guide to the Alpine Plants of New Zealand, John T Salmon (out of print).
New Zealand Alpine Plants, A E Marks and Nancy M Adams (out of print).

Other
Which New Zealand Insect?, Andrew Crowe, 2002.
Whales and Dolphins of New Zealand, Alan N Baker, Victoria University Press, 1983.

OTHER REFERENCE BOOKS
Some of these are guidebooks that are more bulky or too detailed for quick and easy reference while you're out, but are useful for referring to later. Others are simply great reads about New Zealand and its wildlife.

Birds
Where to Watch Birds in New Zealand, Kathy Ombler, New Holland, 2007.
Field Guide to New Zealand Birds, Barrie Heather and Hugh Robertson, Viking, 1996.
Albatrosses, Petrels and Shearwaters of the World, Derek Onley and Paul Scofield, Christopher Helm, 2007.
Identification of Seabirds of the Southern Ocean, Derek Onley and Sandy Bartle, Te Papa Press, 2006.

Plants
New Zealand Ferns and Allied Plants, P J Brownsey and J C Smith-Dodsworrth, David Bateman Ltd, 1992.
The Forest Carpet, Bill and Nancy Malcolm, Timber Press, 1996.
Native Trees of New Zealand, John T Salmon, Reed New Zealand, 2004.
Mosses of New Zealand, Jessica Beever, K W Allison and John Child, University of Otago Press, 1996.
Wetland plants in New Zealand, Peter Johnson and Pat Brooke, Maanaki Whenua Press, 1998.

Geology
A Visitors' Guide to New Zealand's National Parks, Kathy Ombler, New Holland, 2005.
The Reed Field Guide to New Zealand Geology, Jocelyn Thornton, Reed New Zealand, 2003.
New Zealand from the Road: Landforms on the North Island, R H Clark, Heinemann Reed, 1989.

THE BROADER PICTURE
New Zealand: A Natural World Revealed, Tui De Roy and Mark Jones, David Bateman Ltd, 2006.
Back from the Brink: The Fight to Save Our Endangered Birds, Gerard Hutching, Penguin Brink NZ, 2004.
Extinct Birds of New Zealand, Alan Tennyson, Te Papa Press, 2006.
Flight of the Huia, Kerry-Jane Wilson, Canterbury University Press, 2004.
Ghosts of Gondwana, George Gibbs, Craig Potton Publishing, 2006.
Forest Vines to Snow Tussock: The Story of New Zealand Plants, John Dawson, Victoria University Press, 1988.
In Search of Ancient New Zealand, Hamish Campbell and Gerard Hutching, Penguin Books, 2007.
The Penguin History of New Zealand, Michael King, Penguin Books, 2003.

CONTACTS AND ORGANISATIONS

Ark in the Park http://ark.forestandbird.org.nz/SITE_Default/SITE_ark/

Bushy Park www.bushypark.org.nz
Contacts: info@bushypark.org.nz; +64 6 3429879

Department of Conservation www.doc.govt.nz
Contacts: enquiries@doc.govt.nz; +64 4 471 0726

Hinewai – Maurice White Native Forest Trust
Long Bay Rd, RD3, Akaroa 7853, New Zealand; +64 3 304 8501

Karori Wildlife Sanctuary www.sanctuary.org.nz
Contacts: kwst@sanctuary.org.nz; +64 4 920 9200

Maungatautari Ecological Island Trust www.maungatrust.org
Contacts: mail@maungatrust.org; +64 7823 745575

Miranda Shorebird Centre www.miranda-shorebird.org.nz/
Contacts: info@miranda-shorebird.org.nz; +64 9 232 2781

New Zealand Alpine Club www.alpineclub.org.nz
Contacts: Margaret McMahon, margaret@alpineclub.org.nz

Orokonui Ecosanctuary – the Otago Natural History Trust
www.orokonui.org.nz *Contacts:* info@orokonui.org.nz; +64 3 482 1755

Ornithological Society of New Zealand www.osnz.org.nz
Contacts: OSNZEO@slingshot.co.nz (local branch details on website)

QEII National Trust www.openspace.org.nz
Contacts: info@openspace.org.nz; +64 4 472 6626

Royal Forest and Bird Protection Society www.forestandbird.org.nz
Contacts: office@forestandbird.org.nz; +64 4 285 7374 (local branch details on website)

Seaweed Association of New Zealand (SANZ) www.sanz.org.nz
Contacts: seaweed@wave.co.nz; +64 7 862 8424

Supporters of Tiritiri Matangi www.tiritirimatangi.org.nz
Contacts: enquiries@tiritirimatangi.org.nz
Bookings: www.doc.govt.nz/tiritiribunkhouse; +64 9 425 7812

Tawharanui Regional Park
http://www.arc.govt.nz/parks/our-parks/parks-in-the-region/tawharanui/

Wellington Botanical Society www.wellingtonbotsoc.wellington.net.nz
Contacts: juliawhite@paradise.net.nz; +64 4 938 5102

GLOSSARY

Alien Any non-native species introduced into an ecosystem by humans
Alpine Describes the climate and habitat above the tree line
Anther Pollen-bearing part of a stamen
Axil Angle at the junction of a leaf stalk and stem

Bulbil Small plantlet that grows on a fern frond, drops off and becomes self-supporting
Buttress root Large tree root that lies close to or partially above the ground's surface and helps support tree

Calyx Refers to sepals as a whole, usually when joined covering a bud
Cephalothorax Fused head and thorax (upper body) in spiders
Climber Plant that grows by winding its way up another plant or a fixed structure
Crustacean Invertebrate animal with eight or more jointed legs and usually a hard shell. Includes crabs, shrimps and lobsters

Diurnal Active during the daytime – as opposed to nocturnal
Drupe Fleshy fruit containing one or two seeds

Ecosystem The entire animal and plant community of a given area
Endemic Lives naturally only in a given location, or breeds only in that location
Epiphyte/epiphytic Growing on another plant, rock or building

Fellfield Rocky alpine habitat
Frond Complete leaf of fern, including stipe and lamina

Gamete Sex cell which joins with another of opposite sex in sexual reproduction
Gametophyte Plant that produces the gametes

Herbaceous A plant whose leaves and stems die back at the end of the growing season (as distinct from trees and shrubs)
Herbfield Alpine grassland, often with numerous perennial herbaceous plants
Hyphae The underground root-like filaments that comprise the bulk of a fungus

Inflorescence Any arrangement of more than one flower on a single plant
Invasive Describes a successful introduced or alien species that alters an ecosystem

Lahar Mudflow composed of volcanic material and water
Lamina Flattened blade or leafy part of a fern frond
Larva/Larvae Immature of insects that have a pupal stage, such as butterflies

Marsupial A primitive mammal that carries its young in a pouch
Montane Hilly or mountainous
Mustelid A member of the weasel family of mammalian carnivores
Mycelium The underground body of a fungus, comprising numerous hyphae

Native Occurring naturally in a given location; not introduced by man
Nymph Immature insect of kinds that do not have a pupa stage, such as dragonflies

Parthenogenesis Development of an egg without fertilisation
Perennial A herbaceous plant that lives for more than two years (although its flowers and leaves may die back each year)
Petiole Leaf stalk
Pinna Segment of a divided lamina or leaf
Pinnate Having a lamina or leaf divided into pinnae
Pneumataphores Plant roots that grow above ground and can 'breathe'
Pollinator Animal that feeds on nectar and as a result carries pollen from plant to plant, permitting fertilisation to take place

Polyandrous Mating of female with more than one male in any one breeding season

Raceme Inflorescence with central 'stem' and flowers on unbranched stalks
Rhizome Underground stem; may also appear above ground
Rictal hairs/bristles Stiff hairs around the base of some birds' bills, including kiwis

Scree Accumulation of broken and loose rock found in mountainous areas, often at the base of crags or cliffs
Sorus/sori A cluster of two or more sporangia
Spatulate Flattened, spatula- or spoon-shaped
Speculum Coloured patch of feathers on a duck's inner wing
Sporangium Capsule that contains spores
Spore Single-celled reproductive unit in fungi and ferns, similar to seed in flowering plants
Sporophyte Spore-producing plant in ferns and fern allies.
Stamen Male part of flower; produces pollen
Stigma Female part of flower; receives pollen
Stipe Stalk of a frond, also the stem of a mushroom
Stipule Scale-like appendage at base of the stipe, often in pairs
Stolon Lateral or horizontal stem that forms new plant at its tip
Stool Pedestal or trunk of a fern
Succulent Plant adapted to dry conditions, which stores water in its plump, fleshy leaves and stems

Thallus Simple plant body, not split into stems, leaves and such
Thorax Mid-section of insect body, between head and abdomen
Toothed Of leaves, having small spikes or points along the edges
Tree line The altitude at which trees can no longer grow, and forest is replaced with alpine vegetation

Umbel Umbrella-shaped cluster of flowers
Umbellifer Plants with umbels
Ungulate Hoofed grazing mammal, such as goat or deer

COMMON MAORI WORDS
Aroha Love, friendship, compassion, sympathy
Atua Spirit or god

Haka Ceremonial dance; not necessarily a war dance
Hangi Earth oven; meal cooked in an earth oven
Hapu Sub-tribe or clan
Hawaiki Polynesian island, homeland of original Maori

Iwi Tribe, kin

Kia ora Friendly greeting; more than just 'hello'
Kiore Polynesian rat
Koru Uncoiling fern frond – symbol of renewal
Kumara Sweet potato, brought by Maori to New Zealand

Mana Prestige, dignity, power, influence – never self-bestowed
Maori Original settlers, possibly translated as 'the people'. Not used until the arrival of the pakeha.
Mauri Life principle, essence
Moana Ocean

Ngati First word of the name of many Iwi

Pa Maori settlement or village, sometimes fortified
Pakeha Non-Maori, applied to early European settlers. It is not derogatory.
Papa-tu-nuk/Papatuanuku Earth Mother

Rangatira Chief
Rangi/Ranginui The sky, Sky Father
Runanga Assembly, council

Tane Man, Lord, God of the forest and birds; son of Ranginui and Papatuanuku
Tangaroa God of the sea
Tangata whenua People of the land, used to refer to the local Maori people
Tangi Death ceremony or lament
Taonga Treasure or precious thing, especially intangible concepts such as Maori language
Tapu Taboo, forbidden; can refer to sacred land that cannot be entered
Tawhirimatea God of the winds
Te reo The Maori language
Tuahu Sacred place

Urupu Burial ground

Wahi Place
Wai Water
Waka Wooden dugout canoe
Whakapapa Genealogy, ancestral history
Whare House
Whenua Land, ground

Pronunciation: *wh* sounds like a soft *f*; vowels as in French or Spanish.

The banded dotterel is the most widespread of the small waders. TDR